PENGUIN HANDBOOKS

CLASSIC KNITTING FOR COUNTRY LIVING

Jill Jago is an advertising copywriter and publishers' packager. Before moving to London in 1980 she taught creative writing at Plymouth College of Art and Design and worked as a researcher and reporter for Westward Television (now TSW).

Jacque Evans works in the entertainment agency business, representing and managing many household names from television, radio and journalism. She has always had a special interest in knitting and fully recommends it as a relaxing and therapeutic activity.

Jill Jago and Jacque Evans have already published *Knitting Nostalgia* (Penguin Books, 1987).

◆

CLASSIC
KNITTING
— FOR —
COUNTRY
LIVING

◆

JILL JAGO
AND
JACQUE EVANS

PENGUIN BOOKS

To my favourite aunt, the lacemaker
Jane Shotter – Jill Jago

To Lewis Evans, the best father that
any daughter could have, especially for
his encouragement and sense of fair
play. He is always loved – Jacque Evans

BY THE SAME AUTHORS
KNITTING NOSTALGIA

Cover photograph by Jill Furmanovsky

Penguin Books Ltd, Harmondsworth, Middlesex, England
Viking Penguin Inc., 40 West 23rd Street, New York, 10010, USA
Penguin Books Australia Ltd, Ringwood, Victoria, Australia
Penguin Books Canada Ltd, 2801 John Street, Markham, Ontario, Canada L3R 1B4
Penguin Books (NZ) Ltd, 182–190 Wairau Road, Auckland 10, New Zealand

First Published 1987

Copyright © Jill Jago and Jacque Evans, 1987
All rights reserved
Typeset in 9/11 Aldus by
Wyvern Typesetting Ltd, Bristol

Made and printed in Great Britain by
Hazell Watson & Viney Limited
Member of the BPCC Group, Aylesbury, Bucks

CONTENTS

INTRODUCTION

$\mathcal{T}$HE THEME is sport – games, leisure, touring, holidaying, weekending – knitting patterns for pastimes that relieve the pressures of the working week. Looking at these wonderful designs from the romantic twenties and thirties (although one or two have crept in from more recent decades) we feel sure that many of you who knit, or who are knitted for, will welcome this opportunity to express yourselves a little more individually . . . However, you don't have to be an *aficionado* of the tennis club, the icerink or the lacrosse pitch to knit, wear and enjoy these delicious hats, coats, cardigans, sweaters, scarves, gloves, stockings and socks. The man's tennis sweater, certainly the classic twenties cricket pullover and even the thigh-high legwarmers (knitted in any colour you fancy) will all take to city life with tremendous panache. ✔ ✔

Most people, when they think of Cornwall, think of St Ives, Bude and Newquay: at a pinch Mevagissey, Fowey and Polperro. Few have experienced the sheer perfection of Cawsand Bay, Minions, St Dominick, St Neot, St Cleer or Cothele Quay. ✔

So, while this is primarily a knitting book, it also includes a glimpse of undiscovered territory of another kind, the luscious pocket of unparalleled scenery that lies between the western banks of the River Tamar and the eastern edge of Bodmin Moor. We hope you enjoy every aspect of our book. ✔ ✔ ✔ ✔ ✔

SPECIAL NOTES

$\mathcal{T}$HE INSTRUCTIONS for the designs in this book have been transcribed from original patterns issued by Patons and Baldwins between the years 1920 and 1950. The approximate dates of origin are shown with each pattern. In some cases there will be slight differences between the original and the updated versions. Many of the original patterns were designed to be knitted with fine ply wool and fine needles, which was appropriate to a more leisurely age. Modifications – thicker yarn and needles – have been made to these particular patterns to make them more acceptable to the modern knitter. The original dimensions given for some of these designs would appear rather skimpy by modern standards so some minor changes have been made to actual measurements. It is difficult to describe any pattern as 'easy' or 'difficult' – different knitters will have different ideas about these descriptions. Please read right through instructions before commencing work, to make sure that any pattern is within your capability. ✔ ✔ ✔ ✔ ✔ ✔ ✔ ✔

TENSION

Successful results can be achieved only if your tension is accurate. Check your tension, using the yarn and needles specified in the pattern, by knitting a 10cm square in the stitch described in the note on tension given with each pattern. Measure and compare the number of stitches and rows with the correct tension. If you have more rows and stitches than you should, repeat the sample with a larger-size needle – if you have less, try a smaller size. ✔ ✔ ✔ ✔ ✔ ✔ ✔ ✔

Note This is even more vital when selecting an alternative yarn to that specified in the pattern. ✔ ✔ ✔ ✔ ✔ ✔ ✔ ✔ ✔ ✔ ✔ ✔ ✔ ✔ ✔ ✔

METRIC/IMPERIAL CONVERSION

All conversions from centimetres to inches are approximations. ✔ ✔ ✔ ✔ ✔

YARN EQUIVALENTS

If the specified yarns are not available, please take advice from a Patons and Baldwins stockist before proceeding with alternatives. ✔ ✔ ✔ ✔ ✔ ✔ ✔ ✔

MATERIALS

Pair each No. 3¼mm and No. 4mm needles.
Cable needle.

TENSION

On No. 4mm needles, 22 sts and 30 rows to 10cm over stocking stitch.

ABBREVIATIONS

K knit; **P** purl; **st** stitch; **inc** increase; **dec** decrease; **tog** together, **tbl** through back of loops; **sl** slip; **psso** pass slipped stitch over; **C8F** slip next 4 sts on cable needle to front of work, K4, then K4 from cable needle; **C8B** slip next 4 sts on cable needle to back of work, K4, then K4 from cable needle; **cm** centimetres; **mm** millimetres; **MS** main shade; **B** 1st contrast; **C** 2nd contrast.

BACK

With No. 3¼mm needles and MS, cast on 102[108,112,118] sts and work in K1, P1 rib for 7cm.
Next row – Rib 8[3,5,8], (M1, rib 5[6,6,6]) 17 times, M1, rib to end. *120[126,130,136] sts.*

Change to No. 4mm needles and work in patt as follows:
1st row (right side) – K10[13,15,18], *P2, K12; rep from * to last 12[15,17,20] sts, P2, K10[13,15,18] sts.
2nd row – P.
3rd to 6th rows – Rep 1st and 2nd rows twice.
7th row – K10[13,15,18] sts, (P2, K4, C8F, P2, K12) 3 times, P2, K4, C8F, P2, K10[13,15,18] sts.
8th row – P.
9th to 14th rows – Rep 1st to 6th rows.

N E D

MAN'S V-NECKED TENNIS SWEATER

A very special pullover with too much style to leave in the archives.

1 9 3 8

To fit chest				
cm	97	102	107	112
in	38	40	42	44

Garment measures				
cm	97	102	107	112
in	38	40	42	44

Length from top of shoulders				
cm	61	62	63	64
in	24	24½	25	25

Sleeve length, cuff turned back				
cm	47	47	47	47
in	18½	18½	18½	18½

Patons Beehive DK

Main shade (MS)				
50g balls	10	10	10	11
1st contrast (B)				
50g balls	1	1	1	1
2nd contrast (C)				
50g balls	1	1	1	1

15th row – K10[13,15,18], (P2, C8B, K4, P2, K12) 3 times, P2, C8B, K4, P2, K10[13,15,18] sts.
16th row – P.
These 16 rows form patt. **.
Continue in patt until Back measures 38cm, ending with right side facing for next row.

Keeping patt correct, **shape armholes** by casting off 3 sts at beg of next 2 rows, then dec 1 st at each end of next 7 rows. Work 1 row. Now dec 1 st at each end of next and every alt row until 94[98,100,104] sts remain.
Continue straight until Back measures 61[62,63,64]cm, ending with right side facing for next row.

Shape shoulders by casting off 9[10,9,10] sts firmly at beg of next 2 rows, then 9[9,10,10] sts at beg of following 4 rows.
Leave remaining 40[42,42,44] sts on a spare needle.

FRONT

Work as for Back to **.
Continue in patt until 18 rows less than on Back to armhole have been worked, ending with right side facing for next row.

Keeping patt correct, **divide for neck** as follows:
Next row – Patt 57[60,62,65] sts, K2 tog, K1, turn; leave remaining sts on a spare needle.
Continue on these 59[62,64,67] sts for first side as follows:
Next row – P2, patt to end.
Next row – Patt to last 3 sts, K2 tog, K1.
Rep last 2 rows 7 times more. *51[54,56,59] sts.*
Next row – P2, patt to end.

Continue shaping neck and at the same time **shape armhole** as follows:
Next row – Cast off 3 sts, patt to last 3 sts, K2 tog, K1.
Next row – P2, patt to end.
Continue dec at neck as before and *at same time* dec 1 st at armhole edge on next 7 rows, then on following 3[4,5,6] alt rows.
Keeping armhole edge straight, dec at *neck only* as before until 6[7,8,9] sts remain.
Work a few rows straight until Front matches Back to shoulder. Cast off.
With right side facing, rejoin yarn to remaining sts, K1, K2 tog tbl, patt to end.
Complete to match first side, reversing shapings and working K2 tog tbl, for neck decrease.

SLEEVES

With No. 3¼mm needles and MS, cast on 50[52,54,56] sts and work in K1, P1 rib for 12cm.
Place marker 6cm up from cast-on edge.
Next row – Rib 4[5,2,3], (M1, rib 6[6,7,7]) 7 times, M1, rib to end. *58[60,62,64] sts.*

Change to No. 4mm needles and work in patt as follows:
1st row (right side) – K7[8,9,10] sts, (P2, K12) 3 times, P2, K7[8,9,10].
2nd row – P.
3rd to 6th rows – Rep 1st and 2nd rows twice.
7th row – Inc in 1st st, K6[7,0,1] sts, C8F 0[0,1,1] time, P2, K12, P2, K4, C8F, P2, K12, P2, K6[7,8,9], inc in last st.
8th row – P.
9th row – K8[9,10,11] sts, (P2, K12) 3 times, P2, K8[9,10,11] sts.
10th row – P.

11th to 13th rows – Rep 9th and 10th rows once, then 9th row again.
14th row – Inc in 1st st, P to last st, inc in last st.
15th row – K9[10,11,12] sts, P2, K12, P2, C8B, K4, P2, K12, P2, C8B, K1[2,3,4] sts.
16th row – P.

Continue in patt as set, shaping sides by inc 1 st at each end of every 7th row from previous increase, and taking side sts into patt as soon as is possible, until there are 88[90,92,94] sts.

Continue in patt until sleeve seam measures 47cm from marker, ending with right side facing for next row.

Keeping patt correct, **shape top** by casting off 3 sts at beg of next 2 rows, then dec 1 st at each end of next and every alt row until 26 sts remain.
Cast off firmly.

FRONT NECKBAND

With right side facing, No. 4mm needles and B, knit up 70[72,76,78] sts down left side of neck, pick up horizontal loop at centre of V and knit into back of it (mark this st with a coloured thread), knit up 70[72,76,78] sts up right side of neck. *141[145,153,157] sts.*

Next row – P to within 1 st of marked st, sl 1 purlways, P2 tog tbl, psso, P to end.

Next row – K to within 1 st of marked st, sl 1 purlways, K2 tog, psso, K to end.

Rep last 2 rows 5[5,6,6] times more. *117[121,125,129] sts.*

Break off B, join in C, and work a
further 10[10,12,12] rows dec at
centre as before. *97[101,101,105] sts.*
Break off C, join in MS and work
front and back neckband as follows:

Next row – *K1, P1; rep from * to
within 2 sts of marked st, K1, sl 1
purlways, K2 tog, psso, K1, *P1, K1;
rep from * to end; now K across
40[42,42,44] sts from back neck, dec
2 sts evenly. *133[139,139,145] sts.*
Next row – *P1, K1; rep from * to
within 1 st of marked st, sl 1
purlways, P2 tog tbl, psso, *K1, P1;
rep from * to end.

Next row – *K1, P1; rep from * to
within 2 sts of marked st, K1, sl 1
purlways, K2 tog, .psso, K1, *P1, K1;
rep from * to end.
Rep last 2 rows once more.
Now cast off in rib, dec at centre as
before.

TO MAKE UP

Do not press.
Join shoulder, side and sleeve seams;
insert sleeves. Fold cuffs back to
right side at markers.

MATERIALS

Pair each No. 3¼mm and No. 4mm
needles.
1 button.

TENSION

On No. 4mm needles, 22 sts and 30
rows to 10cm over stocking stitch.

ABBREVIATIONS

K knit; **P** purl; **st** stitch; **tog** together;
inc increase; **dec** decrease;
rep repeat; **beg** beginning;
alt alternate; **cm** centimetres;
in inches; **mm** millimetres;
patt pattern; **sl** slip.

BACK

With No. 3¼mm needles, cast on
82[86,92,98] sts and work 2 rows K1,
P1 rib.

Change to No. 4mm needles and,
starting with a K row, work in
stocking stitch until Back measures
14cm, ending with a P row.

Shape sides by inc 1 st at each end
of next and every 10th row, until
there are 90[94,100,106] sts.
Work straight until Back measures
33cm, ending with a P row.

Shape armholes by casting off 3 sts
at beg of next 2 rows, then dec 1 st
at each end of following 5[5,7,7]
rows. Work 1 row.
Now dec 1 st at each end of next and
every alt row until 68[72,74,78] sts
remain.
Work straight until Back measures
52[53,54,55]cm, ending with a P
row.

Shape shoulders by casting off
7[6,7,8] sts at beg of next 2 rows,

CATHERINE

WOMAN'S SINGLE-
BUTTONED
CARDIGAN WITH
WIDE REVER
COLLAR

*All the elegance of a
completely different era
brought right up to
the minute*

1 9 3 4

To fit bust				
cm	81	86	91	97
in	32	34	36	38
Garment measures				
cm	81	86	91	97
in	32	34	36	38
Length from top of shoulders				
cm	51	52	53	54
in	20	20½	21	21½
Sleeve seam				
cm	46	46	47	47
in	18	18	18½	18½

Patons Moorland Tweed DK

50g balls		9	9	10	10

then 6[7,7,7] sts at beg of following
4 rows.
Cast off remaining 30[32,32,34] sts.

RIGHT FRONT

With No. 3¼mm needles, cast on
55[58,61,65] sts and work as follows:
1st row (right side) – K2, *P1, K1;
rep from * to last 1[0,1,1] st,
P1[0,1,1].
2nd row – K1[0,1,1], *P1, K1; rep
from * to end.

Change to No. 4mm needles and
continue as follows:
Next row – K2, (P1, K1)
14[15,15,16] times, P1, K to end.
Next row – P24[25,28,30], *K1, P1;
rep from * to last st, K1.
These 2 rows form patt.
Continue in patt until Front
measures 12cm, ending with right
side facing for next row.

Work buttonhole as follows:
Next 2 rows – Patt 4, cast off 3, patt
to end and back, casting on 3 sts over
those cast off.

Continue in patt until Front
measures 14cm, ending with right
side facing for next row.

Keeping patt correct, **shape side** by
inc 1 st at end of next and every
10th row until there are 59[62,65,69]
sts.

Work in patt until Front measures
33cm, ending with *wrong* side facing
for next row.

Shape armhole by casting off 3 sts
at beg of next row, then dec 1 st at
armhole edge on following 5[5,7,7]
rows. Work 1 row.

Now dec 1 st at armhole edge on next and every alt row until 48[51,52,55] sts remain.
Work in patt until Front matches Back to shoulder, ending with *wrong* side facing for next row.

Shape shoulder by casting off 7[6,7,8] sts at beg of next row, then 6[7,7,7] sts at beg of following 2 alt rows. *29[31,31,33] sts.*
Next row – Patt to end, cast on 18[20,20,22] sts. *47[51,51,55] sts.*
Next row – K1, *P1, K1; rep from * to end.
Next row – K2, *P1, K1; rep from * to last st, P1.
Next 2 rows – Patt 42, turn, sl 1, patt to end.
Next 2 rows – Patt 36, turn, sl 1, patt to end.

Next 2 rows – Patt 30, turn, sl 1, patt to end.
Next 2 rows – Patt 24, turn, sl 1, patt to end.
Next 2 rows – In patt across all sts. Cast off loosely in rib.

LEFT FRONT

With No. 3¼mm needles, cast on 55[58,61,65] sts and work as follows:
1st row (right side) – P1[0,1,1], *K1, P1; rep from * to last 2 sts, K2.
2nd row – *K1, P1; rep from * to last 1[0,1,1] st, K1[0,1,1].

Change to No. 4mm needles and continue as follows:
Next row – K24[25,28,30], *P1, K1; rep from * to last st, K1.

Next row – K1, (P1, K1) 15[16,16,17] times, P to end.
These 2 rows form patt.
Work to correspond with Right Front, omitting buttonhole and reversing shapings.
(**Note:** You will end *right* side facing for next row for armhole and shoulder shapings.)

SLEEVES

With No. 3¼mm needles, cast on 42[44,44,46] sts and work in K1, P1 rib for 7cm, inc 4 sts evenly across last row. *46[48,48,50] sts.*

Change to No. 4mm needles and, starting with a K row, work in stocking stitch, shaping sides by inc 1 st at each end of 7th[7th,9th,9th] and every following 11th[11th,10th,10th] row until there are 66[68,70,72] sts. Work straight until sleeve seam measures 46[46,47,47]cm, ending with a P row.

Shape top by casting off 3 sts at beg of next 2 rows, then dec 1 st at each end of next and following 2nd[4th,4th,4th] row. Work 1[1,1,3] rows.
Now dec 1 st at each end of next and every alt row until 20 sts remain. Cast off.

TO MAKE UP

With wrong side of work facing, block each piece by pinning out round edges and, omitting ribbing, press parts lightly following instructions on the yarn labels.
Join shoulder, side and sleeve seams. Insert sleeves. Join centre back collar seam, then sew cast on collar edge to back neck.
Press seams.

MATERIALS

Pair No. 4mm needles.
No. 3.50mm crochet hook.
6 buttons.

TENSION

On No. 4mm needles, 22 sts and 30 rows to 10cm over patt.

ABBREVIATIONS

K knit; **P** purl; **st** stitch; **inc** increase; **dec** decrease; **beg** beginning; **alt** alternate; **rep** repeat; **patt** pattern; **cm** centimetres; **in** inches; **mm** millimetres; **dc** double crochet.

BACK

With No. 4mm needles and main shade cast on 99[105,111,117,123] sts and work in patt as follows:
1st row (right side) – K3, *P3, K3; rep from * to end.
2nd row – Purl.
3rd row – P3, *K3, P3; rep from * to end.
4th row – Purl.
These 4 rows form patt.
Continue in patt until 100 rows have been worked, ending with right side facing for next row.

Keeping continuity of patt, **shape armholes** by casting off 6[6,6,7,7] sts at beg of next 2 rows.
Dec 1 st at each end of next and every alt row until 73[75,77,81,83] sts remain.
Work straight until Back measures 55[55,56,57,58]cm, ending with right side facing for next row.

Shape shoulders by casting off 7 sts at beg of next 4 rows, then 6[7,7,8,8] sts at beg of following 2

J A N E T

WOMAN'S DOUBLE-BREASTED WAISTCOAT

For cruising around or just to take the chill off summer evenings. This little waistcoat works equally well with skirts, shorts or trousers.

1 9 2 7

To fit bust					
cm	81	86	91	97	102
in	32	34	36	38	40

Garment measures					
cm	89	94	99	105	110
in	35	37	39	41½	43½

Length from shoulder					
cm	55	55	56	57	58
in	21½	21½	22	22½	23

Patons Cotton Perlé

Main shade					
50g balls		7	7	8	8	8
Contrast					
50g balls		1	1	1	1	1

rows. Cast off remaining 33[33,35,37,39] sts.

RIGHT FRONT

With No. 4mm needles and main shade cast on 3 sts and shape point as follows:
1st row (right side) – P3.
2nd and every alt row – Cast on 3 sts, P across these sts, P to last st, inc in last st.
3rd row – Inc in first st, K3, P3.
5th row – Inc in first st, K2, P3, K3, P3.
7th row – Inc in first st, K1, (P3, K3) twice, P3.
9th row – Inc in first st, (P3, K3) 3 times, P3.
11th row – Inc in first st, P2, (K3, P3) 4 times.
13th row – Inc in first st, P1, (K3, P3) 5 times.
15th row – Inc in first st, (K3, P3) 6 times.
17th row – Inc in first st, K2, (P3, K3) 6 times, P3.
19th row – Inc in first st, K1, (P3, K3) 7 times, P3.
21st row – Inc in first st, (P3, K3) 8 times, P3.
23rd row – Inc in first st, P2, (K3, P3) 9 times.

1st and 2nd sizes only

Next row – Cast on 3[6] sts, P across these sts, P to last st, inc in last st. *62[65] sts.*

3rd, 4th and 5th sizes only

25th row – Inc in first st, P1, (K3, P3) 10 times.
27th row – Inc in first st, (K3, P3) 11 times.

3rd and 4th sizes only

Next row – Cast on 3[6] sts, P across these sts, P to last st, inc in last st. *72[75] sts.*

5th size only

29th row – Inc in first st, K2, (P3, K3) 11 times, P3.
31st row – Inc in first st, K1, (P3, K3) 12 times, P3.
Next row – Cast on 3 sts, P across these sts, P to last st, inc in last st. *82 sts.*

All sizes

Keeping continuity of patt, inc 1 st at *beginning* of next row and at the same edge on following 9[9,5,5,1] rows taking inc sts into patt. *72[75,78,81,84] sts.*
Work 4 rows in patt.
** **Next row** (buttonhole) – Patt 5, cast off 2, patt 31 (including st on needle after cast off), cast off 2, patt to end.

Next row – Patt to end, casting on over those cast off. ***.
Work 36 rows in patt. **.
Now rep from ** to ** once more, then rep from ** to *** once.
Work 2 rows in patt.

Shape front slope by dec 1 st at *beginning* of next and every alt row until 63[66,69,72,75] sts remain, ending with wrong side facing for next row.

Keeping continuity of patt, **shape armhole** and continue shaping front slope as follows:
Next row – Cast off 6[6,6,7,7] sts, patt to end.
Dec 1 st at each end of next and

every alt row until 43[42,41,43,42] sts remain. Work 1 row.
Now dec 1 st at front slope *only* on next and every alt row until 20[21,21,22,22] sts remain.
Work straight until Front matches Back to start of shoulder shaping, ending with wrong side facing for next row.

Shape shoulder by casting off 7 sts at beg of next and following alt row.
Work 1 row.
Cast off remaining 6[7,7,8,8] sts.

LEFT FRONT

With No. 4mm needles and main shade, cast on 3 sts and shape point as follows:
1st row (right side) – P3.
2nd and every alt row – Inc in first st, P to end, cast on 3 sts.
3rd row – P3, K3, inc in last st.
5th row – P3, K3, P3, K2, inc in last st.
7th row – (P3, K3) twice, P3, K1, inc in last st.
9th row – (P3, K3) 3 times, P3, inc in last st.
11th row – (P3, K3) 4 times, P2, inc in last st.
13th row – (P3, K3) 5 times, P1, inc in last st.
15th row – (P3, K3) 6 times, inc in last st.
17th row – (P3, K3) 6 times, P3, K2, inc in last st.
19th row – (P3, K3) 7 times, P3, K1, inc in last st.
21st row – (P3, K3) 8 times, P3, inc in last st.
23rd row – (P3, K3) 9 times, P2, inc in last st.

1st and 2nd sizes only

Next row – Inc in first st, P to end,

cast on 3[6] sts. *62[65] sts.*

3rd, 4th and 5th sizes only

25th row – (P3, K3) 10 times, P1, inc in last st.
27th row – (P3, K3) 11 times, inc in last st.

3rd and 4th sizes only

Next row – Inc in first st, P to end, cast on 3[6] sts. *72[75] sts.*

5th size only

29th row – (P3, K3) 11 times, P3, K2, inc in last st.
31st row – (P3, K3) 12 times, P3, K1, inc in last st.
Next row – Inc in first st, P to end, cast on 3 sts. *82 sts.*

All sizes

Keeping continuity of patt, inc 1 st at *end* of next row and at the same edge on following 9[9,5,5,1] rows, taking inc sts into patt. *72[75,78,81,84] sts.*
Work 84 rows in patt.

Shape front slope by dec 1 st at *end* of next and every alt row until 64[67,70,73,76] sts remain, ending with right side facing for next row.

Keeping continuity of patt, **shape armholes** and continue shaping front slope as follows:
Next row – Cast off 6[6,6,7,7] sts, patt to last 2 sts, work 2 tog.
Work 1 row.
Dec 1 st at each end of next and every alt row until 43[42,41,43,42] sts remain. Work 1 row.
Now dec 1 st at front slope only on next and every alt row until 20[21,21,22,22] sts remain.

Work straight until Front matches Back to start of shoulder shaping, ending with right side facing for next row.

Shape shoulder by casting off 7 sts at beg of next and following alt row. Work 1 row.
Cast off remaining 6[7,7,8,8] sts.

TO MAKE UP

Press on wrong side of work, following instructions on yarn label. Join shoulder and side seams.
With 3.50mm crochet hook and main shade, start at side seam and work all round edge in dc, slip stitch to first dc.
Next round – In contrast, work 1 dc into each dc all round edge, (working 2 dc into 1 dc at front points), slip stitch to first dc.
Now work a further 2 rounds in contrast and 1 round in main shade. Work in same way round each armhole.
Sew on buttons to correspond with buttonholes.

MATERIALS

Beret: 1 50g ball **Patons Cotton Perlé** in main shade and 1 50g ball in contrast.
Scarf: 1 50g ball **Patons Cotton Perlé** in main shade and 1 50g ball in contrast.
Pair No. 4mm needles.

MEASUREMENTS

Beret: to fit average woman's head.
Scarf: length approx 122cm (48in).

TENSION

On No. 4mm needles, 22 sts and 29 rows to 10cm over stocking stitch.

ABBREVIATIONS

K knit; **P** purl; **sts** stitches;
tog together; **inc** increase;
dec decrease; **beg** beginning;
alt alternate; **rep** repeat; **patt** pattern;
cm centimetres; **in** inches;
mm millimetres; **yfwd** yarn forward;
yrn yarn round needle; **sl 1** slip one stitch; **psso** pass slipped stitch over.

BERET

Cast on 39 sts in main shade and work in patt as follows:
1st row – K1, K2 tog, K16, yfwd, K1, yfwd, K16, K2 tog, K1.
2nd row – K1, P2 tog, P16 yrn, P1, yrn, P16, P2 tog, K1.
3rd row – As 1st.
4th row – As 2nd.
5th row – As 2nd.

6th row – As 1st.
7th row – As 2nd.
8th row – As 1st.
Rep 1st to 8th rows 6 times more, then 1st to 4th rows again. Break off main shade, join in contrast and rep

FLORA

**WOMAN'S BERET
AND SCARF
MATCHED WITH
JANET**

*In silky cotton
yarn, this lacy
cap-and-scarf duo is
quick to knit and
pretty enough
to add flair to lots of
different outfits.*

1 9 2 9

5th to 8th rows once, then 1st to 8th rows 7 times.
Cast off.

With right side facing join main shade and **knit up** 89 sts evenly along side edge.
1st row (wrong side) – K1, *P1, K1; rep from * to end.
2nd row – P1, *K1, P1; rep from * to end.
Rep these 2 rows 4 times more, then 1st row again.
Next row – P1, *sl 1, K2 tog, psso, K1; rep from * to end. *45 sts.*
Rep 1st and 2nd rows twice more, then 1st row again.
Next row – P1, *sl 1, K2 tog, psso, K1; rep from * to end. *23 sts.*
Rep 1st and 2nd rows once more, then 1st row again.

Next row – P1, *sl 1, K1, psso; rep from * to end. Break yarn, thread through remaining 12 sts, draw up tightly and fasten off securely.

With right side facing, join main shade to other edge and **knit up** 89 sts evenly along edge.
1st row (wrong side) – P1, *K1, P1; rep from * to end.
2nd row – K1, *P1, K1; rep from * to end.
Rep these 2 rows 3 times more, then 1st row again. Cast off in rib.

TO MAKE UP

Do not press. Join seam.

SCARF

Cast on 37 sts in MS and work in patt as follows:
1st row – K1, K2 tog, K15, yfwd, K1, yfwd, K15, K2 tog, K1.
2nd row – K1, P2 tog, P15, yrn, P1, yrn, P15, P2 tog, K1.
3rd row – As 1st.
4th row – As 2nd.
5th row – As 2nd.

6th row – As 1st.
7th row – As 2nd.
8th row – As 1st.
Rep 1st to 8th rows 6 times more. Break off main shade; join contrast and shape as follows:
1st row – K18, yfwd, K1, yfwd, K18.
2nd row – K1, P2 tog, P16, yrn, P1, yrn, P16, P2 tog, K1.

3rd row – K1, K2 tog, K16, yfwd, K1, yfwd, K16, K2 tog, K1.
4th and 5th rows – As 2nd.
6th row – As 3rd.
7th row – K1, P18, yrn, P1, yrn, P18, K1.

8th and 9th rows – K1, K2 tog, K17, yfwd, K1, yfwd, K17, K2 tog, K1.

10th row – K1, P2 tog, P17, yrn, P1, yrn, P17, P2 tog, K1.

11th row – As 8th.

12th row – As 10th.

13th row – K1, P19, yrn, P1, yrn, P19, K1.

14th row – K1, K2 tog, K18, yfwd, K1, yfwd, K18, K2 tog, K1.

15th row – K1, P2 tog, P18, yrn, P1, yrn, P18, P2 tog, K1.

16th row – As 14th.

Break off contrast; join in main shade.

17th and 18th rows – As 14th and 15th.

19th row – K21, yfwd, K1, yfwd, K21.

Break off main shade; join in contrast.

20th and 21st rows – K1, P2 tog, P19, yrn, P1, yrn, P19, P2 tog, K1.

22nd row – K1, K2 tog, K19, yfwd, K1, yfwd, K19, K2 tog, K1.

23rd row – As 20th.

24th row – As 22nd.

Break off contrast; join in main shade.

25th row – K22, yfwd, K1, yfwd, K22.

26th row – K1, P2 tog, P20, yrn, P1, yrn, P20, P2 tog, K1

27th row – K1, K2 tog, K20, yfwd, K1, yfwd, K20, K2 tog, K1.

28th and 29th rows – As 26th.

30th row – As 27th.

31st row – K1, K22, yfwd, P1, yrn, P22, K1.

32nd row – K1, K2 tog, K21, yfwd, K1, yfwd, K21, K2 tog, K1.

Break off main shade; join in contrast.

33rd row – As 32nd.

34th row – K1, P2 tog, P21, yrn, P1, yrn, P21, P2 tog, K1.

35th row – As 32nd.

36th row – As 34th.

37th row – K1, P23, yrn, P1, yrn, P23, K1. *51 sts.*

38th row – K1, K2 tog, K22, yfwd, K1, yfwd, K22, K2 tog, K1.

39th row – K1, P2 tog, P22, yrn, P1, yrn, P22, P2 tog, K1.

Cast off knitways.

Work a second piece in same way.

GUSSET

Cast on 2 sts in main shade.

Work in garter stitch (every row K), shaping by inc 1 st at each end of next and every alt row until there are 22 sts. Work 1 row.

Now dec 1 st at each end of next and every alt row until 2 sts remain.

Work 2 tog.

TO MAKE UP

Do not press.

Sew gusset in position between the two pieces at centre back of scarf.

MATERIALS

Pair each No. 3¼ and No. 4½mm
needles.
Cable needle.

TENSION

On No. 4½mm needles, 19 sts and
25 rows to 10cm over stocking stitch.

ABBREVIATIONS

K knit; **P** purl; **sts** stitches;
tog together; **tbl** through back of
loop; **inc** increase; **dec** decrease;
M1 make a stitch by picking up
horizontal loop lying before next
stitch and working into back of it;
C4F slip next 2 sts on cable needle to
front of work, K next 2 sts tbl, then
K 2 sts from cable needle tbl;
patt pattern; **rep** repeat;
beg beginning; **cm** centimetres;
in inches; **mm** millimetres.

BACK

With No. 3¼mm needles, cast on
82[92,102] sts and work in K1, P1 rib
for 4cm.
Next row – Rib 3[8,6] , (M1, rib
5[5,6]) 15 times, M1, rib to end.
98[108,118] sts.

Change to No. 4½mm needles and
work in patt as follows:
1st row (right side) – P0[0,2],
K2[0,2], P2[1,2], *K1, P2, K1 tbl 4
times, P2, K1, P2, K2, P2; rep from
* to last 14[11,16] sts, K1, P2, K1 tbl
4 times, P2, K1, P2[1,2], K2[0,2],
P0[0,2].

2nd row – K0[0,2], P2[0,2], K2[1,2],
*P1, K2, P1 tbl 4 times, K2, P1, K2,
P2, K2; rep from * to last 14[11,16]
sts, P1, K2, P1 tbl 4 times, K2, P1,
K2[1,2], P2[0,2], K0[0,2].
3rd row – K0[0,2], P2[0,2], K2[1,2],

LINDSAY

HIS AND HERS
ARAN-STYLE
SWEATER

*A streamlined
version of a
traditional pattern;
more elegant than
the familiar
chunky Aran.*

1 9 5 9

To fit bust/chest			
cm	86–91	97–102	107–112
in	34–36	38–40	42–44

Garment measures			
cm	96	107	117
in	38	42	46

Length from top of shoulders			
cm	65	67	69
in	25½	26½	27

Sleeve seam			
cm	46	47	48
in	18	18½	19

Patons Diploma Aran

50g balls	14	16	18

*K1, P2, C4F, P2, K3, P2, K2; rep
from * to last 14[11,16] sts, K1, P2,
C4F, P2, K3[2,3], P2[0,2], K0[0,2].
4th row – P0[0,2], K2[0,2], P2[1,2],
*P1, K2, P1 tbl 4 times, K2, P3, K2,
P2; rep from * to last 14[11,16] sts,
P1, K2, P1 tbl 4 times, K2, P3[2,3],
K2[0,2], P0[0,2].

5th row – As 1st.
6th row – As 2nd.
7th row – K0[0,2], P2[0,2], K2[1,2],
*K1, P2, K1 tbl 4 times, P2, K3, P2,
K2; rep from * to last 14[11,16] sts,
K1, P2, K1 tbl 4 times, P2, K3[2,3],
P2[0,2], K0[0,2].
8th row – As 4th.
These 8 rows form patt.
Continue in patt until Back measures
42cm, ending with right side facing
for next row.

Keeping patt correct, **shape raglans**
by casting off 3 sts at beg of next 2
rows.
Next row – K1, K2 tog tbl, patt to
last 3 sts, K2 tog, K1.
Next row – K1, P1, patt to last 2 sts,
P1, K1. ******
Rep last 2 rows until 40[48,54] sts
remain, ending with right side facing
for next row.

Next row – K1, K3 tog tbl, patt to
last 4 sts, K3 tog, K1.
Next row – K1, P1, patt to last 2 sts,
P1, K1.
Rep last 2 rows 1[2,3] times more.
32[36,38] sts.
Leave sts on a spare needle.

FRONT

Work as for Back to ******.
Rep last 2 rows until 52[60,66] sts
remain, ending with right side facing
for next row.

Continue shaping raglan and **divide for neck** as follows:
1st row – K1, K2 tog tbl, patt 14[16,18], work 2 tog, turn and leave remaining sts on a spare needle.
Continue on these 17[19,21] sts for first side as follows:
2nd row – Work 2 tog, patt to last 2 sts, P1, K1.
3rd row – K1, K2 tog tbl, patt to last 2 sts, work 2 tog.
Rep 2nd and 3rd rows once more.

Next row – Patt to last 2 sts, P1, K1.
Next row – K1, K2 tog tbl, patt to last 2 sts, work 2 tog.
Rep last 2 rows once more.
Next row – Patt to last 2 sts, P1, K1.
Next row – K1, K2 tog tbl, patt to end.
Next row – Patt to last 2 sts, K1, P1.

Next row – K1, K3 tog tbl, patt to end.
Rep last 2 rows 0[1,2] times more.
Next row – Patt 2, P1, K1.
Next row – K1, K3 tog tbl.
Next row – P1, K1.
K2 tog and fasten off.

With right side of work facing, leave centre 14[18,20] sts on a length of yarn, work 2 tog, patt to last 3 sts, K2 tog, K1.

Complete to correspond with first side, reversing shapings and working K2 tog and K3 tog in place of K2 tog tbl and K3 tog tbl at raglan shaping.

SLEEVES

With No. 3¼mm needles, cast on 42[44,48] sts and work in K1, P1 rib for 6cm.
Next row – Rib 3[4,1], (M1, rib 5[4,5]) 7[9,9] times, M1, rib to end. *50[54,58] sts.*

Change to No. 4½mm needles and place patt as follows:
1st row (right side) – K1 tbl 3[0,0] times, P2[0,1], K1[0,1], *P2, K2, P2, K1, P2, K1 tbl 4 times, P2, K1; rep from * to last 12[6,8] sts, P2, K2, P2, K1[0,1], P2[0,1], K1 tbl 3[0,0] times.

2nd row – P1 tbl 3[0,0] times, K2[0,1], P1[0,1], *K2, P2, K2, P1, K2, P1 tbl 4 times, K2, P1; rep from * to last 12[6,8] sts, K2, P2, K2, P1[0,1], K2[0,1], P1 tbl 3[0,0] times.

3rd row – K1 tbl 3[0,0] times, P2[0,1], K1[0,1], *K2, P2, K3, P2, C4F, P2, K1; rep from * to last 12[6,8] sts, K2, P2, K2, K1[0,1], P2[0,1], K1 tbl 3[0,0] times.

4th row – P1 tbl 3[0,0] times, K2[0,1], P1[0,1], *P2, K2, P3, K2, P1 tbl 4 times, K2, P1; rep from * to last 12[6,8] sts, P2, K2, P2, P1[0,1], K2[0,1], P1 tbl 3[0,0] times.
5th row – As 1st.
6th row – As 2nd.
7th row – K1 tbl 3[0,0] times, P2[0,1] K1[0,1], *K2, P2, K3, P2, K1 tbl 4 times, P2, K1; rep from * to last 12[6,8] sts, K2, P2, K2, K1[0,1], P2[0,1], K1 tbl 3[0,0] times.

8th row – As 4th.
These 8 rows form patt.
Continue in patt, shaping sides by inc 1 st at each end of next [3rd,3rd] and every following 10th[8th,7th] row until there are 68[76,84] sts, taking inc sts into patt.

Work straight until sleeve seam measures 46[47,48]cm, ending with right side facing for next row.

Keeping patt correct, **shape top** by casting off 3 sts at beg of next 2 rows.
Next row – K1, K2 tog tbl, patt to last 3 sts, K2 tog, K1.
Next row – K1, P1, patt to last 2 sts, P1, K1.
Rep last 2 rows until 6[14,18] sts remain, ending with right side facing for next row.

2nd and 3rd sizes only

Next row – K1, K3 tog tbl, patt to last 4 sts, K3 tog, K1.

Next row – K1, P1, patt to last 2 sts, P1, K1.
Rep last 2 rows 1[2] times. *6 sts.*

All sizes

Leave these 6 sts on a safety-pin.

TO MAKE UP

With wrong side of work facing, block each piece by pinning out round edges and, omitting ribbing, press parts lightly following instructions on yarn label, taking care not to spoil patt.
Join front raglan seams and right back raglan seam.

NECKBAND

With right side facing and No. 3¼mm needles, K 6 sts from left sleeve, knit up 16[18,20] sts down left side of neck, K14[18,20] sts from centre, dec 1 st at centre, knit up 16[18,20] sts up right side, K 6 sts from right sleeve, then K32[36,38] sts from back, dec 3 sts evenly across back. *86[98,106] sts.*
Work in K1, P1 rib for 5cm. Cast off loosely in rib.
Join neckband and remaining raglan seam, then join side and sleeve seams.
Fold neckband in half to wrong side and slip hem loosely in position all round.

MATERIALS

Pair each No. 3¼mm and No. 4mm needles.

TENSION

On No. 4mm needles, 22 sts and 29 rows to 10cm over stocking stitch.

ABBREVIATIONS

K knit; **P** purl; **sts** stitches; **tog** together; **inc** increase; **dec** decrease; **M1** make a stitch by picking up the horizontal loop lying before the next stitch and working into the back of it; **beg** beginning; **rep** repeat; **alt** alternate; **cm** centimetres; **in** inches; **mm** millimetres; **MS** main shade; **C** contrast.

NOTE

When working stripes on collar, twist yarns on wrong side when changing colour to avoid a hole.

BACK

With No. 3¼mm needles and MS, cast on 92[98,104,110,116] sts and work 4cm in K1, P1 rib, inc 4 sts evenly across last row.
96[102,108,114,120] sts.

Change to No. 4mm needles and work as follows:
1st row – In MS, K.
2nd row – In MS, P.
3rd row – In C, K.
4th row – In C, P.
5th to 8th rows – Rep 1st to 4th rows.
Break off C.
Continue in MS and stocking stitch until Back measures 42[42,42,43,43]cm, ending with a P row.

S U S A N

SAILOR WOMAN'S SHORT-SLEEVED JUMPER WITH SAILOR COLLAR

A neat, eye-catching sweater – watch heads turn as you breeze along the quay.

1 9 5 2

To fit bust

cm	81	86	91	97	102
in	32	34	36	38	40

Garment measures

cm	87	92	98	103	109
in	34	36	38½	40½	43

Length from top of shoulders

cm	60	61	62	63	64
in	23½	224	24½	25	25

Sleeve seam, with cuff turned back

cm	15	15	16	16	17
in	6	6	6½	6½	½

Patons Cotton Soft

Main shade 50g balls	10	10	11	11	12
Contrast 50g balls	1	1	1	1	1

Shape armholes by casting off 4 sts at beg of next 2 rows.
88[94,100,106,112] sts. **.**
Continue straight until back measures 60[61,62,63,64]cm, ending with a P row.
Cast off.

FRONT

Work as for Back to **.
Continue straight until Front measures 45[46,46,47,48]cm, ending with a P row.

Divide for neck as follows:
Next row – K42[45,48,51,54] sts, K2 tog, turn and leave remaining sts on a spare needle.

Continue on these 43[46,49,52,55] sts for first side and dec 1 st at neck edge on following 4[6,6,8,11] alt rows, then on every following 3rd row until 29[31,33,35,37] sts remain. Work a few rows straight if required until Front matches Back to shoulder. Cast off.

With right side facing, rejoin MS yarn to remaining sts, K2 tog, K to end.
Finish to correspond with first side, reversing shapings.

SLEEVES

With No. 3¼mm needles and MS, cast on 50[52,54,54,56] sts and work 4 rows in K1, P1 rib.

Change to No. 4mm needles and work in stripes as 1st to 8th rows on Back. Break off C.
Continue in MS and work a further 6 rows stocking stitch, ending with a P row. Mark this row with a coloured thread at each end.
Starting with a P row, continue in

stocking stitch for 17 rows.
Now **shape sides** by inc 1 st at each end of next and every alt row until there are 74[78,82,82,86] sts. Work straight until sleeve seam measures 17[17,18,18,19]cm from markers, ending with a P row.

Shape top by casting off 9[9,10,10,10] sts at beg of next 6 rows. Cast off remaining sts.

COLLAR

Divide C yarn into two balls, and make a spare, small ball of MS yarn. With No. 3¼mm needles and MS cast on 76[80,86,90,96] sts and K 3 rows.

Change to No. 4mm needles and work as follows:
1st row (right side) – K.
2nd row – K2, P to last 2 sts, K2.
3rd row – K3 in MS, with first ball of C K70[74,80,84,90] sts in C, with spare ball of MS K3 in MS.
4th row – K2 in MS, P1 in MS, P72[76,82,86,92] sts in C, P1 in MS, K2 in MS.
5th row – K3 in MS, K2 in C, K66[70,76,80,86] sts in MS, with second ball of C K2 in C, K3 in MS.
6th row – K2 in MS, P1 in MS, P2 in C, P66[70,76,80,86] sts in MS, P2 in C, P1 in MS, K2 in MS.

7th row – K3 in MS, K2 in C, K2 in MS, with first ball of C K62[66,72,76,82] sts in C, using spare ball of MS K2 in MS, with second ball of C K2 in C, K3 in MS.

8th row – With spare ball of MS, K2 in MS, P1 in MS, P2 in C, P2 in MS, with main ball of C P62[66,72,76,82] sts in C, with main ball of MS P2 in MS, P2 in C, P1 in MS, K2 in MS. Break off spare ball of MS.
9th row – K3 in MS, K2 in C, K2 in MS, K2 in C, K58[62,68,72,78] sts in MS, K2 in C, K2 in MS, K2 in C, K3 in MS.

10th row – K2 in MS, P1 in MS, P2 in C, P2 in MS, P2 in C, P58[62,68,72,78] sts in MS, P2 in C, P2 in MS, P2 in C, P1 in MS, K2 in MS.
Rep 9th and 10th rows until collar measures 17[17,17,18,18]cm, ending with *wrong* side facing for next row.

Next row – Patt 23[24,26,27,29] sts, cast off the next 30[32,34,36,38] sts, patt to end.
Continue on the first 23[24,26,27,29] sts for left front of collar as follows:

4th and 5th sizes only

Continue in patt, dec 1 st at neck edge on next and following 3[6] alt rows. Work 2 rows.

All sizes

Continue in patt, dec 1 st at neck edge on next and every 3rd row until 10 sts remain.
Work 7[4,0,0,7] rows straight, ending with right side facing for next row. Break off C.
Continue in MS as follows:

1st row – K.
2nd row – K2, P6, K2.
3rd row – K2, M1, K to last 2 sts, M1, K2.
4th row – K2, P to last 2 sts, K2.
5th row – K.
6th to 12th rows – Rep 4th and 5th rows 3 times, then 4th row again. Rep 3rd to 12th rows twice more, then 3rd row again. *18 sts.*
Work a few rows straight until work measures 14cm from point where C yarn was broken off, ending with right side facing for next row.
Work 2 rows in C, 2 rows in MS, and 2 rows in C. Break off C.
Work a further 2 rows in MS.

Change to No. 3¼mm needles and K 3 rows. Cast off.

With right side facing, rejoin appropriate yarn to second group of sts and work to correspond with left front collar, reversing shapings.

COLLAR TAB

With No. 3¼mm needles and MS, cast on 4 sts and work in garter stitch (every row K) for 4cm.
Cast off.

TO MAKE UP

Do not press.
Join shoulder seams. Sew sleeve tops along armhole edges of back and front, then join a few rows at each side of sleeves to cast off armhole sts. Join side and sleeve seams, turn cuffs at marked points to right side. Sew neck edge of collar neatly to neck edge of sweater. Place collar tab around ties of collar as in colour photograph and join cast-on and cast-off edges of tab, placing join underneath collar ties.

MATERIALS

Pair each No. 3¼mm and No. 4mm needles.
Cable needle.

TENSION

On No. 4mm needles, 22 sts and 30 rows to 10cm stocking stitch.

ABBREVIATIONS

K knit; **P** purl; **st** stitch; **tog** together; **tbl** through back of loops; **inc** increase; **dec** decrease; **M1** make a stitch by picking up horizontal loop lying before next stitch and working into back of it; **patt** pattern; **rep** repeat; **beg** beginning; **alt** alternate; **C8F** slip next 4 sts on cable needle to front of work, K4, then K4 from cable needle; **C8B** slip next 4 sts on cable needle to back of work, K4, then K4 from cable needle; **cm** centimetres; **in** inches; **mm** millimetres.

FRONT

With No. 3¼mm needles, cast on 84[90,96,102] sts and work in K1, P1 rib for 10cm.
Next row – (Rib 3, M1) 9[12,15,14] times, (rib 2[2,2,4], M1) 14[8,2,4] times, (rib 3, M1) 9[12,15,14] times, rib 2. *116[122,128,134] sts.*

Change to No. 4mm needles and work in patt as follows:
1st row (right side) – P4[5,8,9], (K12, P12[13,13,14]) 4 times, K12, P4[5,8,9].
2nd row – K4[5,8,9], (P12, K12[13,13,14]) 4 times, P12, K4[5,8,9].
3rd and 4th rows – As 1st and 2nd.
5th row – P4[5,8,9], (C8F, K4, P12[13,13,14]) 4 times, C8F, K4, P4[5,8,9].

GILDA

WOMAN'S V-NECKED CABLE SWEATER

Fly a kite, walk the dog or just laze away an early autumn afternoon.

1 9 3 6

To fit bust				
cm	79–81	84–86	89–91	94–97
in	31–32	33–34	35–36	37–38

Garment measures				
cm	81	86	91	97
in	32	34	36	38

Length from top of shoulders				
cm	53	54	55	56
in	21	21½	21½	22

Sleeve seam				
cm	44	44	44	44
in	17½	17½	17½	17½

Patons Beehive DK

50g balls				
		7	7	8	8

6th to 10th rows – Rep 2nd row once, then 1st and 2nd rows twice more.
11th row – P4[5,8,9], (K4, C8B, P12[13,13,14]) 4 times, K4 C8B, P4[5,8,9].
12th row – As 2nd.
These 12 rows form patt.
Continue in patt until Front measures approximately 34cm, ending with 6th or 12th row of patt. ******.

Keeping patt correct, place neck ribbing as follows:
1st row – Patt 52[55,58,61], (K1, P1) twice, K4, (P1, K1) twice, patt to end.
2nd row – Patt 52[55,58,61] sts, (P1, K1) 3 times, (K1, P1) 3 times, patt to end.
3rd row – As 1st.
4th row – As 2nd.

Divide for neck and shape armhole as follows:
5th row – Cast off 3 sts, patt 48[51,54,57], including st on needle after cast off, K2 tog, P1, K1, P1, K2.
6th row – (K1, P1) 3 times, patt to end.
7th row – Work 2 tog, patt to last 7 sts, K2 tog, P1, K1, P1, K2.
8th row – (K1, P1) 3 times, patt to last 2 sts, work 2 tog.
Rep last 2 rows 3[4,5,5] times more, then 7th row again.

Next row – (K1, P1) 3 times, patt to end.
Next row – Work 2 tog, patt to last 7 sts, K2 tog, P1, K1, P1, K2.
Rep last 2 rows 3[3,3,4] times.
Next row – (K1, P1) 3 times, patt to end.
Next row – Work 2 tog, patt to last 6 sts, (K1, P1) twice, K2.
Next row – (K1, P1) 3 times, patt to end.

Next row – Patt to last 7 sts, K2 tog, P1, K1, P1, K2.
Next row – (K1, P1) 3 times, patt to end.
Next row – Patt to last 6 sts, (K1, P1) twice, K2.
Rep last 4 rows until 24[24,24,25] sts remain.
Continue straight in patt until armhole measures 18[19,20,21]cm, ending with right side facing for next row.

Shape shoulder by casting off 8[8,8,9] sts at beg of next row, then 8 sts at beg of following 2 rows.

With right side facing, rejoin yarn to remaining sts and work as follows:
1st row – K2, P1, K1, P1, K2 tog tbl, patt to end.
2nd row – Cast off 3 sts, patt to last 6 sts, (P1, K1) 3 times.
3rd row – K2, P1, K1, P1, K2 tog tbl, patt to last 2 sts, work 2 tog.
4th row – Work 2 tog, patt to last 6 sts, (P1, K1) 3 times.
Rep last 2 rows 3[4,5,5] times more, then 4th row again.
Next row – Patt to last 6 sts, (P1, K1) 3 times.
Next row – K2, P1, K1, P1, K2 tog tbl, patt to last 2 sts, work 2 tog.
Rep last 2 rows 3[3,3,4] times.
Next row – Patt to last 6 sts, (P1, K1) 3 times.
Next row – K2, (P1, K1) twice, patt to last 2 sts, work 2 tog.
Next row – Patt to last 6 sts, (P1, K1) 3 times.
Next row – K2, P1, K1, P1, K2 tog tbl, patt to end.
Next row – Patt to last 6 sts, (P1, K1) 3 times.
Next row – K2, (P1, K1) twice, patt to end.
Rep last 4 rows until 24[24,24,25] sts remain.

Finish as for first side, reversing shapings.

BACK

Work as for Front to **.
Work a further 4 rows in patt.

Shape armholes by casting off 3 sts at beg of next 2 rows, then dec 1 st at each end of next 9[11,13,13] rows. Work 1 row.
Now dec 1 st at each end of next and following 4[4,4,5] alt rows.
82[84,86,90] sts.
Continue straight in patt until Back matches Front to shoulder, ending with right side facing for next row.

Shape shoulders and work back neck edge as follows:
1st row – Cast off 8[8,8,9] sts, patt 10[10,10,10], including st on needle after cast off, (P1, K1) 9[9,10,11] times, (P1, K2 tog) 3 times, (P1, K1) 9[10,10,10] times, P1, patt to end.
2nd row – Cast off 8[8,8,9] sts, patt 10[10,10,10], including st on needle after cast off, K1, (P1, K1) 21[22,23,24] times, patt to end.
3rd row – Cast off 8 sts, patt 2, including st on needle after cast off, P1, (K1, P1) 21[22,23,24] times, patt to end.
4th row – Cast off 8 sts, patt 2, including st on needle after cast off, K1, (P1, K1) 21[22,23,24] times, patt 2.
5th row – Cast off 8, rib to last 2 sts, patt 2.
6th row – Cast off 8, rib to end.
Cast off remaining 31[33,35,37] sts.

SLEEVES

With No. 3¼mm needles, cast on 42[44,44,46] sts and work in K1, P1 rib for 6cm.
Next row – Rib 4[5,5,6], (M1, rib 2) 17 times, M1, rib to end.
60[62,62,64] sts.

Change to No. 4mm needles and work in patt as follows:
1st row (right side) – K12, (P12[13,13,14], K12) twice.
2nd row – P12, (K12[13,13,14], P12) twice.
3rd and 4th rows – As 1st and 2nd.
5th row – C8F, K4, (P12[13,13,14], C8F, K4) twice.
6th to 8th rows – Rep 2nd row, then 1st and 2nd rows once more.
9th row – Inc in first st, K11, P12[13,13,14], K12, P12[13,13,14], K11, inc in last st.
10th row – K1, (P12, K12[13,13,14]) twice, K12, K1.
11th row – P1, (K4, C8B, P12[13,13,14]) twice, K4, C8B, P1.
12th row – As 10th.
Continue in patt as set, shaping sides by inc 1 st at each end of every 11th[11th,10th,10th] row from previous inc, until there are 78[80,82,84] sts, taking inc sts into reverse stocking stitch.
Work straight until sleeve seam measures 44cm, ending with right side facing for next row.

Keeping patt correct, **shape top** by casting off 3 sts at beg of next 2 rows, then dec 1 st at each end of next and every alt row until 42[42,38,38] sts remain, ending with right side facing for next row.
Now dec 1 st at each end of every row until 28 sts remain.
Next row – Work 2 tog, patt 6, (P2 tog, P1) 4 times, patt 6, work 2 tog.
Cast off remaining sts.

TO MAKE UP

Do not press.
Join shoulder, side and sleeve seams.
Insert sleeves.

N E T T A

**WOMAN'S
PATTERN-BANDED
SWEATER**

*Plaids or tartan-
style checks blend
beautifully with
this brilliant sweater.
Watch its
personality change
with different
colour contrasts.*

1 9 2 0

MATERIALS

Pair each No. 3¼mm, No. 4mm and
No. 4½mm needles.

TENSION

On No. 4mm needles, 22 sts and 30
rows to 10cm over stocking stitch.

ABBREVIATIONS

K knit; **P** purl; **sts** stitches;
tog together; **inc** increase;
dec decrease; **M1** make a stitch by
picking up horizontal loop lying
before next stitch and working into
back of it; **patt** pattern; **rep** repeat;
alt alternate; **cm** centimetres;
in inches; **mm** millimetres; **MS** main
shade; **B** 1st contrast; **C** 2nd contrast;
D 3rd contrast.

NOTE

When working in patt from chart,
read odd rows P from right to left
and even rows K from left to right.
Strand yarns loosely across back of
work over not more than 3 sts at a
time to keep fabric elastic.

BACK

With No. 3¼mm needles and B, cast
on 92[96,102,108] sts and work 2
rows K1, P1 rib. Break off B, join in
C.
Next row (right side) – K.
Next row – *K1, P1; rep from * to
end. Break C, join in MS.
Next row – K. **.
Now continue in K1, P1 rib until
back measures 7cm, ending with
wrong side facing for next row.
Next row – Rib 8[3,6,9], (M1, rib
5[6,6,6]) 15 times, M1, rib to end.
108[112,118,124] sts.

To fit bust

cm	81	86	91	97
in	34	36	38	38

Garment measures

cm	97	102	107	112
in	38	40	42	44

Length of top of shoulders

cm	64	65	66	67
in	25	25½	26	26½

Sleeve seam, with cuff turned back

cm	44	44	45	45
in	17½	17½	17½	17½

Patons Clansman DK

Main shade (MS)				
50g balls		8	8	9	9
1st contrast (B)				
50g balls		3	3	3	4
2nd contrast (C)				
50g balls		2	2	2	2
3rd contrast (D)				
50g balls		1	1	1	1

Change to No. 4mm needles and,
joining in and breaking off colours as
required, work in patt as follows:
1st row – In B, K.
2nd row – In B, P.
3rd row – In D, K.
4th row – In C, P.
5th row – In C, K.
6th row – In MS, P.
7th row – In MS, K.

8th to 15th rows – Using No. 4½
mm needles, work 8 rows in patt
from chart (see p. 36), rep 10 patt
sts 10[11,11,12] times across row,
and first and last 4[1,4,2] sts on each
row as indicated.

Change to No. 4mm needles and
continue as follows:
16th row – In MS, P.
17th row – In MS, K.
18th row – In C, P.
19th row – In C, K.
20th row – In D, P.
21st row – In B, K.
22nd row – In B, P.
23rd to 34th rows – In MS, work in
stocking stitch.
These 34 rows form patt. ***.
Continue in patt until Back measures
64[65,66,67]cm, ending with right
side facing for next row.

Shape shoulders by casting off
12[13,13,15] sts at beg of next 2
rows, then 13[13,14,14] sts at beg of
following 4 rows. Leave remaining
32[34,36,38] sts on a spare needle.

FRONT

Work as for Back to ***.
Continue in patt until Front
measures 58[59,60,61]cm, ending
with a P row.

Keeping patt correct, **divide for neck** as follows:

Next row – Patt 44[45,47,49] sts, K2 tog, turn and leave remaining sts on a spare needle.

Continue on these 45[46,48,50] sts for first side and dec 1 st at neck edge on next 4 rows.

Work 1 row.

Now dec 1 st at neck edge on next and following 2 alt rows. *38[39,41,43] sts.*

Work a few rows straight until Front matches Back to shoulder, ending with a P row.

Shape shoulder by casting off 12[13,13,15] sts at beg of next row, then 13[13,14,14] sts at beg of following 2 alt rows.

With right side facing, leave centre 16[18,20,22] sts on a length of yarn, rejoin appropriate colour yarn to remaining sts, K2 tog, patt to end. Finish to match first side reversing shapings.

SLEEVES

With No. 3¼mm needles and B, cast on 48[48,50,50] sts and work in rib

as for Back to **.

Continue in rib until cuff measures 14cm, ending with right side facing for next row.

Next row – Rib 4[1,5,8] sts, (M1, rib 3[3,3,2]) 13[15,13,17] times, M1, rib to end. *62[64,64,66] sts.*

Change to No. 4mm needles and work in patt as for Back, starting with 29th[27th,25th,25th] row and shaping sides by inc 1 st at each end of 9th[5th,7th,7th] row and every following 7th row until there are 88[92,92,96] sts, taking inc sts into patt.

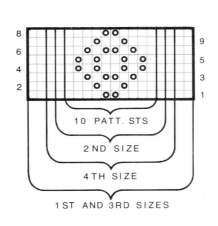

10 PATT. STS

2ND SIZE

4TH SIZE

1ST AND 3RD SIZES

KEY

☐ = M S

◙ = B

NOTE

When working patt from chart the first time, rep the 10 patt sts 6[6,6,7] times across row, and first and last 2[4,4,1] sts on each row as indicated. Work a few rows straight until sleeve seam measures 51[51,52,52]cm. Cast off.

TO MAKE UP

With wrong side of work facing, block each piece by pinning out round edges and, omitting ribbing, press parts lightly following instructions on yarn label. Join right shoulder seam.

POLO COLLAR

With right side facing, No. 3¼mm needles and MS, knit up 22 sts down left side of neck, K16[18,20,22] sts from centre, inc 4 sts evenly, knit 22 sts up right side, then K32[34,36,38] sts from back, inc 8 sts evenly. *104[108,112,116] sts.*
Work in K1, P1 rib for 13cm, ending with right side facing (noting collar turns over to right side) for next row. Break MS, join in C.

Next row – K.
Next row – In rib, break off C and join in B.
Next row – K.
Next row – In rib.
Cast off evenly in rib.

Join collar and left shoulder seam. Place centre of sleeve tops to shoulder seams, then sew sleeve tops to side edges of back and front. Join side and sleeve seams.
Press seams.
Turn back cuffs and turn down polo collar.

MATERIALS

Pair each No. 3¼mm and No. 4mm needles.

TENSION

On No. 4mm needles, 19 sts and 30 rows to 10cm over stocking stitch.

ABBREVIATIONS

K knit; **P** purl; **st** stitch; **tog** together; **tbl** through back of loops; **inc** increase; **dec** decrease; **beg** beginning; **alt** alternate; **rep** repeat; **patt** pattern; **cm** centimetres; **in** inches; **mm** millimetres; **M1** make a stitch by picking up horizontal loop lying before next stitch and working into back of it; **MS** main shade (Sahara); **C** contrast (Cotton Perlé).

NOTE

When working colour patt use separate balls of yarn, twisting yarn on wrong side of work when changing colour to avoid a hole.

FRONT

** With No. 3¼mm needles and MS, cast on 77[83,87,93] sts and work in rib as follows.
1st row (right side) – K1, *P1, K1; rep from * to end.
2nd row – P1, *K1, P1; rep from * to end.
Rep these 2 rows until rib measures 7[8,8,8]cm, ending with a 2nd row, and inc 1 st at centre of last row. *78[84,88,94] sts.*

Change to No. 4mm needles.
Starting with a K row, work 12 rows in stocking stitch.

A L I C E

V-NECK
SLEEVELESS
PATTERNED
SWEATER

Typically twenties design, knitted in contrasting yarns and colours.

1 9 2 8

To fit bust				
cm	81	86	91	97
in	32	34	36	38

Garment measures				
cm	81	86	91	97
in	32	34	36	38

Length from shoulder				
cm	53	55	56	57
in	21	21½	22	22½

Patons Sahara

Main shade	50g balls	4	4	5	5

Patons Cotton Perlé

Contrast	50g balls	1	1	1	1

Joining in and breaking off colours as required, work in patt as follows:
1st row (right side) – In C, K.
2nd row – In C, P.
3rd to 6th rows – In MS, as 1st and 2nd rows twice.
7th row – K0[3,5,8] in C, *K6 in MS, K12 in C; rep from * to last 6[9,11,14] sts, K6 in MS, K0[3,5,8] in C.
8th row – P0[3,5,8] in C, *P6 in MS, P12 in C; rep from * to last 6[9,11,14] sts, P6 in MS, P0[3,5,8] in C.

9th to 20th rows – As 7th and 8th rows 6 times.
21st to 24th rows – In MS as 1st and 2nd rows twice.
25th to 28th rows – In C, as 1st and 2nd rows twice.
29th row – K0[0,2,5] in C, K9[12,12,12] in MS, *K6 in C, K12 in MS; rep from * to last 15[18,20,23] sts, K6 in C, K9[12,12,12] in MS, K0[0,2,3] in C.

30th row – P0[0,2,3] in C, P9[12,12,12] in MS, *P6 in C, P12 in MS; rep from * to last 15[18,20,23] sts, P6 in C, P9[12,12,12] in MS, P0[0,2,3] in C.

31st to 42nd rows – As 29th and 30th rows 6 times.
43rd to 46th rows – In C as 1st and 2nd rows twice.
47th to 50th rows – In MS as 1st and 2nd rows twice.
51st and 52nd rows – In C as 1st and 2nd rows.
Break off C and continue in MS only.
Starting with a K row, work 14 rows in stocking stitch **.

Now continue as follows:
1st row – K2, (P1, K1) 4 times, K to last 10 sts, (K1, P1) 4 times, K2.
2nd row – (K1, P1) 5 times, P to last 10 sts, (P1, K1) 5 times. Rep 1st and 2nd rows once more, then 1st row again.
6th row – (K1, P1) 5 times, P29[32,34,37] sts, M1, P29[32,34,37] sts, (P1, K1) 5 times. *79[85,89,95] sts.*

Shape armhole as follows:
1st row – Cast off 2, K1, (P1, K1) 3 times, K22[25,27,30], P1, (K1, P1) 7 times, K22[25,27,30], (K1, P1) 4 times, K2.
2nd row – Cast off 2, P1, (K1, P1) 3 times, P22[25,27,30], K1, (P1, K1) 7 times, P22[25,27,30], (P1, K1) 4 times.

3rd row – K2, (P1, K1) 3 times, K2 tog tbl, K20[23,25,28], P1, (K1, P1) 7 times, K20[23,25,28], K2 tog, (K1, P1) 3 times, K2.
4th row – (K1, P1) 4 times, P21[24,26,29], K1, (P1, K1) 7 times, P21[24,26,29], (P1, K1) 4 times.

5th row – K2, (P1, K1) 3 times, K2 tog tbl, K19[22,24,27], P1, (K1, P1) 7 times, K19[22,24,27], K2 tog, (K1, P1) 3 times, K2.
6th row – (K1, P1) 4 times, P20[23,25,28], (K1, P1) 3 times, K1, K2 tog, (P1, K1) 3 times,

P20[23,25,28], (P1, K1) 4 times. *70[76,80,86] sts.*

Divide for V neck as follows:
1st row – K2, (P1, K1) 3 times, K2 tog tbl, K15[18,20,23], K2 tog, (K1, P1) 3 times, K2, turn. Leave remaining sts on a spare needle.
2nd row – (K1, P1) 4 times, P to last 8 sts, (P1, K1) 4 times.

3rd row – K2, (P1, K1) 3 times, K2 tog tbl, K to last 8 sts, (K1, P1) 3 times. K2.
4th row – As 2nd row.
5th row – K2, (P1, K1) 3 times, K2 tog tbl, K to last 10 sts, K2 tog, (K1, P1) 3 times, K2.
Rep the last 4 rows 1[2,2,3] times more.
*** Keeping continuity of rib at each end, dec 1 st at front slope *only* as before on every following 4th row from previous dec until 23[24,25,25] sts remain.

Work straight until Front measures 53[55,56,57]cm, ending with right side facing for next row.

Shape shoulder by casting off 5[6,6,6] sts at beg of next and following alt row. Work 1 row. Cast off 6[5,6,6], rib to end. Continue in rib on remaining 7 sts until strip measures approx 7[7,8,8]cm. Cast off in rib.

With right side facing, rejoin yarn to remaining sts. K2, (P1, K1) 3 times, K2 tog tbl, K15[18,20,23], K2 tog, (K1, P1) 3 times, K2.
Continue as follows:

1st row – (K1, P1) 4 times, P to last 8 sts, (P1, K1) 4 times.
2nd row – K2, (P1, K1) 3 times, K to last 10 sts, K2 tog, (K1, P1) 3 times, K2.
3rd row – As 1st row.
4th row – K2, (P1, K1) 3 times, K2 tog tbl, K to last 10 sts, K2 tog, (K1, P1) 3 times, K2.
Rep last 4 rows 1[2,2,3] times more. Now complete to match first side from *** to end, reversing shapings.

BACK

Work as given for Front from ** to **.
1st row – K2, (P1, K1) 4 times, K to last 10 sts, (K1, P1) 4 times, K2.

Alice

2nd row – (K1, P1) 5 times, P to last 10 sts, (P1, K1) 5 times. Rep last 2 rows twice more.

Shape armholes as follows:
1st row – Cast off 2, K1, (P1, K1) 3 times, K to last 10 sts, (K1, P1) 4 times, K2.
2nd row – Cast off 2, P1, (K1, P1) 3 times, P to last 8 sts, (P1, K1) 4 times.
3rd row – K2, (P1, K1) 3 times, K2 tog tbl, K to last 10 sts, K2 tog, (K1, P1) 3 times, K2.

4th row – (K1, P1) 4 times, P to last 8 sts, (P1, K1) 4 times. Rep 3rd and 4th rows only until 60[62,66,68] sts remain.

Keeping continuity of rib at each end, work straight until Back measures same as Front to start of shoulder shaping, ending with right side facing for next row.

Shape shoulders by casting off 5[6,6,6] sts at beg of next 4 rows, then 6[5,6,6] sts at beg of following 2 rows. Cast off remaining 28[28,30,32] sts.

TO MAKE UP

Do not press.
Join shoulder and side seams. Sew rib strips across back neck and join short edges.

MATERIALS

Pair each No. 3¼mm and No. 4mm needles.

TENSION

On No. 4mm needles, 20 sts and 29 rows to 10cm over stocking stitch.

ABBREVIATIONS

K knit; **P** purl; **sts** stitches; **tog** together; **tbl** through back of loop; **inc** increase; **dec** decrease; **beg** beginning; **alt** alternate; **rep** repeat; **patt** pattern; **cm** centimetres; **in** inches; **mm** millimetres; **A** shade A (Cotton Perlé); **B** shade B (Cotton Splash).

NOTE

When working colour patt use separate balls of yarn, twisting yarn on wrong side of work when changing colour to avoid a hole.

BACK

** With No. 3¼mm needles and A, cast on 83[89,93,99] sts and work in rib as follows:
1st row (right side) – K1, *P1, K1; rep from * to end.
2nd row – P1, *K1, P1; rep from * to end.
Rep these 2 rows for 7[7,8,8]cm, ending with a 2nd row, inc 1 st at centre of last row. *84[90,94,100] sts.* **.

Change to No. 4mm needles.
Starting with a K row, work 28 rows in stocking stitch.
Break off A, join in B and work in 48 rows in stocking stitch, ending with a P row.

D E L I A

V-NECK
SLEEVELESS
PATTERNED
SWEATER

High summer design – pretty by day, easy to dress up for balmy evenings.

1 9 2 8

To fit bust				
cm	81	86	91	97
in	32	34	36	38
Garment measures				
cm	84	89	94	100
in	33	35	37	39½
Length from shoulder				
cm	53	54	56	57
in	21	21½	22	22½
Patons Cotton Perlé				
Shade A 50g balls	2	2	3	3
Patons Cotton Splash				
Shade B 50g balls	4	4	5	5

Shape armholes by casting off 6 sts at beg of next 2 rows.
Dec 1 st at each end of next and following 3[5,5,7] alt rows. *64[66,70,72] sts.*
Work straight until armhole measures 20[21,22,23]cm, ending with a P row.

Shape shoulders by casting off 6 sts at beg of next 4 rows, then 5[6,7,7] sts at beg of following 2 rows.
Cast off remaining 30[30,32,34] sts.

FRONT

Work as given for Back from ** to **.

Change to No. 4mm needles.
Joining in B as required work as follows:
1st row (right side) – K40[43,45,48] in A, 4 in B, 40[43,45,48] in A.
2nd row – P40[43,45,48] in A, 4 in B, 40[43,45,48] in A.
3rd and 4th rows – As 1st and 2nd.
5th row – K39[42,44,47] in A, 6 in B, 39[42,44,47] in A.
6th row – P39[42,44,47] in A, 6 in B, 39[42,44,47] in A.
7th and 8th rows – As 5th and 6th.
9th row – K38[41,43,46] in A, 8 in B, 38[41,43,46] in A.
10th row – P38[41,43,46] in A, 8 in B, 38[41,43,46] in A.
11th and 12th rows – As 9th and 10th.
13th row – K37[40,42,45] in A, 10 in B, 37[40,42,45] in A.
14th row – P37[40,42,45] in A, 10 in B, 37[40,42,45] in A.
15th and 16th rows – As 13th and 14th.

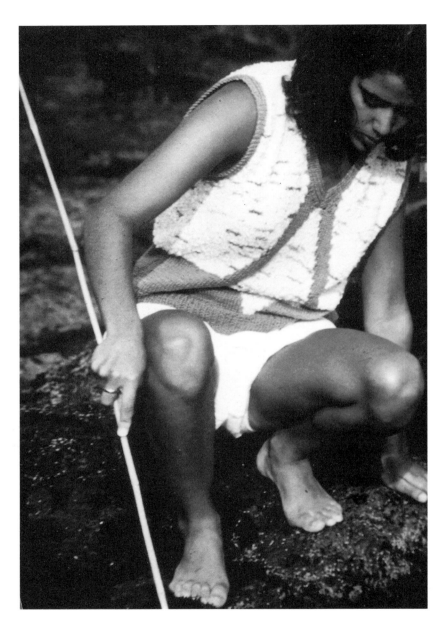

17th row – K36[39,41,44] in A, 12 in B, 36[39,41,44] in A.
18th row – P36[39,41,44] in A, 12 in B, 36[39,41,44] in A.
19th and 20th rows – As 17th and 18th.
21st row – K28[31,33,36] in A, 28 in B, 28[31,33,36] in A.

22nd row – P28[31,33,36] in A, 28 in B, 28[31,33,36] in A.
23rd and 24th rows – As 21st and 22nd.
25th row – K29[32,34,37] in A, 26 in B, 29[32,34,37] in A.
26th row – P29[32,34,37] in A, 26 in B, 29[32,34,37] in A.

27th and 28th rows – As 25th and 26th.
29th row – K24[27,29,32] in B, 6 in A, 24 in B, 6 in A, 24[27,29,32] in B.
30th row – P24[27,29,32] in B, 6 in A, 24 in B, 6 in A, 24[27,29,32] in B.

31st and 32nd rows – As 29th and 30th.

Continue to move the 6 sts in A towards the centre by working 1 st *more* in B at each side and 2 sts *less* in B at centre on next and every following 4th row until the row

K35[38,40,43] in B, 6 in A, 2 in B, 6 in A, and 35[38,40,43] in B has been worked.

Next row – P35[38,40,43] in B, 6 in A, 2 in B, 6 in A, 35[38,40,43] in B.
Next row – K35[38,40,43] in B, 6 in A, 2 in B, 6 in A, 35[38,40,43] in B.

Divide for neck as follows:
Next row – P35[38,40,43] in B, 6 in A, cast off 2 sts, P6 in A (including st on needle after cast off), P35[38,40,43] in B.
Work on last 41[44,46,49] sts for first side, leaving remaining sts on a spare needle.

Shape armhole and neck as follows:
1st row – Cast off 6 sts K30[33,35,38] in B (including st on needle after cast off), (K2, K2 tog, K1) in A.
2nd row – P4 in A, P to end in B.
3rd row – K2 tog, K29[32,34,37] in B, 4 in A.
4th row – P4 in A, P to end in B.
5th row – K2 tog, K28[31,33,36] in B, K2 tog, K1 in A.
6th row – P2 in A, P to end in B.
7th row – K2 tog, K27[30,32,35] in B, K2 in A.

8th row – As 6th.
Break off A.

Continue in B only, dec 1 st at armhole edge on next and following 0[2,2,4] alt rows only, *at the same time* dec 1 st at neck edge as before on next and every following 4th row until 17[18,19,19] sts remain.
Work straight until Front matches Back to start of shoulder shaping, ending with a P row.

Shape shoulder by casting off 6 sts at beg of next and following alt row.
Work 1 row.
Cast off remaining 5[6,7,7] sts.

With right side facing rejoin A to remaining sts; K1, K2 tog tbl, K2 in A, K to end in B.

Shape armhole and neck:
Next row – Cast off 6 sts, P30[33,35,38] in B (including st on needle after cast off), P4 in A.
Finish to correspond with first side, reversing shapings.

NECK BORDER

With No. 3¼mm needles and A, cast on 2 sts.
1st row – Inc in first st, K1.
2nd row – K3.
3rd row – Inc in first st, P1, K1.
4th row – K2, P1, K1.
5th row – Inc in first st, K1, P1, K1.
6th row – K2, P1, K2.
7th row – Inc in first st, (P1, K1) twice.
8th row – K2, (P1, K1) twice.
9th row – Inc in first st, (K1, P1) twice, K1.
10th row – K2, (P1, K1) twice, K1.
11th row – Inc in first st (P1, K1) 3 times. *8 sts.*
12th row – K2, (P1, K1) 3 times.
13th row – (P1, K1) 4 times.

Rep last 2 rows until strip measures approx 48[51,53,56]cm along shortest edge, ending with the 12th row.
Now dec 1 st at beg of next and every alt row until 2 sts remain.
Cast off.

ARMHOLE BORDERS

With No. 3¼mm needles and A, cast on 8 sts.
1st row – K2, (P1, K1) 3 times.
Rep this row until strip fits round armhole. Cast off in rib.

TO MAKE UP

Do not press.
Join shoulder and side seams. Join mitred ends of neck border and sew in position round neck. Sew armhole borders in position.

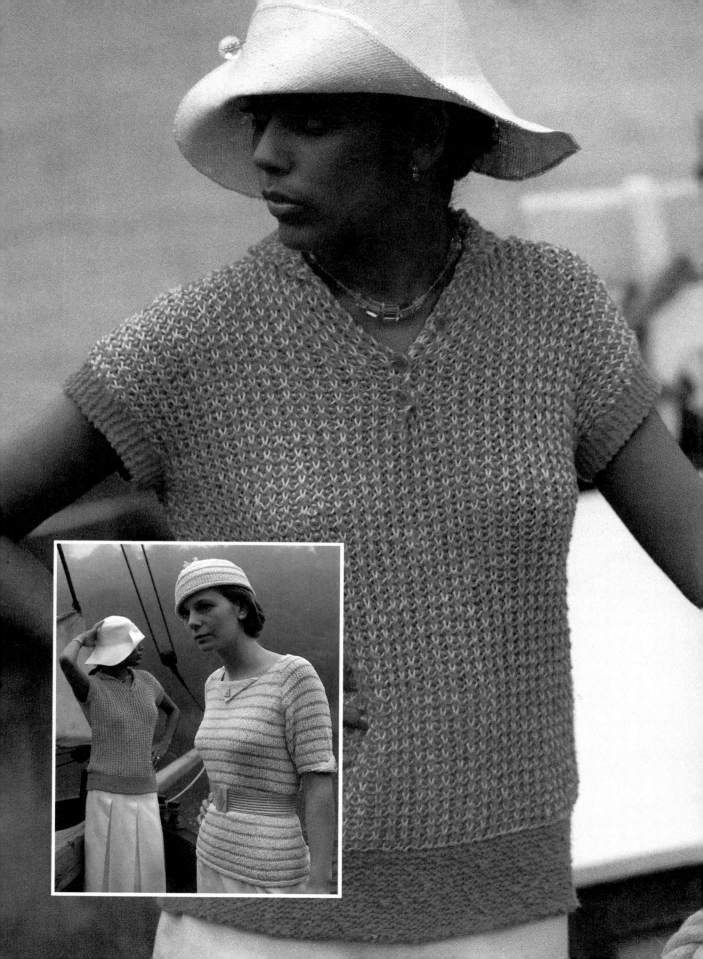

MATERIALS

Pair each No. 4mm and No. 5mm needles.
6 small buttons.

TENSION

On No. 5mm needles, 17 sts and 34 rows to 10cm over patt.

ABBREVIATIONS

K knit; **P** purl; **st** stitch; **yfwd** yarn forward; **beg** beginning; **alt** alternate; **rep** repeat; **patt** pattern; **cm** centimetres; **mm** millimetres; **in** inches; **MS** main shade (Cotton Top); **C** contrast (Cotton Perlé); **sl 1** slip one stitch.

BACK

** With No. 4mm needles and MS, cast on 72[76,80,84] sts and work 10cm in garter stitch (every row K).
Change to No. 5mm needles, join in C and work in patt as follows:
1st row – In C, *K1, yfwd, sl 1 purlways; rep from * to last 2 sts, K2.
2nd row – In C, K1, * yfwd, sl 1 purlways, K tog the next st and the yfwd of the previous row; rep from * to last st, K1.
Rep 2nd row only twice using MS, and 2nd row twice using C. These 4 rows form patt.
Continue in patt until Back measures approx 58[58,59,60]cm, ending with the 2nd row of C.

NOTE

When casting off always count the next st and yfwd of previous row as one stitch.

Keeping continuity of patt, **shape shoulders** as follows:

EVELINE

WOMAN'S COTTON JUMPER

Light, bright and quickly knitted in two colours, a popular little summer jumper from the thirties.

1 9 2 5

To fit bust				
cm	81	86	91	97
in	32	34	36	38

Garment measures				
cm	85	89	94	99
in	33½	35	37	39

Length from top of shoulders				
cm	61	61	62	63
in	24	24	24½	25

Patons Cotton Top				
Main shade 50g balls	4	4	5	5

Patons Cotton Perlé				
Contrast 50g balls	3	3	3	4

Cast off 4 sts at beg of next 12[10,6,4] rows.

2nd, 3rd and 4th sizes only

Cast off 5 sts at beg of following 2[6,8] rows.

All sizes

Leave remaining 24[26,26,28] sts on a spare needle.

FRONT

Work as given for Back from ** until Front measures approx 44[44,45,46]cm, ending with the 2nd row of C.
Divide for front opening as follows:
Next row – In MS, patt 36[38,40,42], turn and leave remaining sts on a spare needle. Continue in patt on the 36[38,40,42] sts until work measures same as Back to start of shoulder shaping, ending with the 2nd row of C.

*** **Shape shoulder** as follows:
Cast off 4 sts at beg of next and following 5[4,2,1] alt rows. Work 1 row.

2nd, 3rd and 4th sizes

Cast off 5 sts at beg of next and following 0[2,3] alt rows. Work 1 row. ***.

All sizes

Leave remaining 12[13,13,14] sts on a spare needle.

With right side facing rejoin MS to remaining sts, patt to end.
Continue in patt until work measures

same as Back to start of shoulder shaping, ending with the 1st row of MS. Work as given for first side of shoulder shaping from *** to ***.

All sizes

Do not break off yarn; leave sts on a spare needle.
Join shoulder seams.

COLLAR

With right side of work facing, slip the 12[13,13,14] sts at right side of front neck on to No. 5mm needle; using MS, patt across 24[26,26,28] sts of Back, then patt across 12[13,13,14] sts at left side of front neck. *48[52,52,56] sts.*
Keeping continuity of patt, work 8cm.
Cast off loosely.

TO MAKE UP – ARMHOLE BORDERS

Do not press.
Join side seams, leaving 17[18,19,20]cm open for armhole.

ARMHOLE BORDERS

With No. 4mm needles and MS, cast on 7 sts and work in garter st (every row K) until strip when slightly stretched fits all round armhole. Sew in position as you go along.
Cast off. Join cast-on and cast-off edges at underarm.
Sew 3 pairs of buttons to front opening evenly spaced. Make a chain link and attach to one side to make a button loop.
Fold collar to right side.

CHRISSIE

WOMAN'S SHORT-
SLEEVED SUMMER
SWEATER AND HAT

*Irresistibly feminine
sweater with
buttoned collar and
cuffs and an appealing
bobblecap.*

1   9   3   4

Sweater

To fit bust

cm	81	86	91	97
in	32	34	36	38

Garment measures

cm	84	90	94	101
in	33	35½	37	40

Length from top of shoulders

cm	57	58	59	60
in	22½	23	23	23½

Sleeve seam (approx)

cm	13	13	13	13
in	5	5	5	5

Patons Sahara

50g balls		7	7	8	8

Patons Cotton Perlé

50g balls		2	2	2	3

Hat

2 50g balls **Patons Sahara**
1 50g ball **Patons Cotton Perlé**

MATERIALS

Pair each No. 3¼mm and No. 4mm
needles.
3 buttons.

TENSION

On No. 4mm needles, 19 sts and 30
rows to 10cm over stocking stitch
using Sahara.

ABBREVIATIONS

K knit; **P** purl; **st** stitch; **inc** increase;
dec decrease; **tog** together;
patt pattern; **rep** repeat;
beg beginning; **alt** alternate;
cm centimetres; **in** inches;
mm millimetres; **MS** main shade
(Sahara); **C** contrast (Cotton Perlé).

NOTE

Carry yarn not in use loosely up side
of work.

SWEATER

BACK

With No. 3¼mm needles and MS,
cast on 77[83,87,93] sts and work 5
rows garter st (every row K), inc 3
sts evenly on last row. *80[86,90,96]
sts.*

Change to No. 4mm needles and
work in stripe patt as follows:
1st row – In C, K.
2nd row – In C, P.
3rd row – In MS, K.
4th row – In MS, P.
5th to 8th rows – Rep 3rd and 4th
rows twice.

These 8 rows form patt.
Continue in patt until Back measures
38cm, ending with a P row.
Continuing in patt, **shape raglans**
by casting off 3 sts at beg of next 2

rows, then dec 1 st at each end of
next and every 4th row until
64[70,76,84] sts remain. Work 1
row. ******.
Now dec 1 st at each end of next and
every alt row until 26[28,28,30] sts
remain, ending with a P row.
With MS, K 2 rows, then cast off
knitways.

FRONT

Work as for Back to ******.
Now dec 1 st at each end of next and
every alt row until 44[46,48,50] sts
remain, ending with a P row.
Continue shaping raglan and **divide
for neck** as follows:
Next row – K2 tog, K9[9,10,10],
turn and leave remaining sts on a
spare needle.
Continue on these 10[10,11,11] sts
for first side as follows:
Next row – K2, P to end.
Next row – K2 tog, K to end.
Rep last 2 rows until 2 sts remain.
Next row – K2.
K2 tog and fasten off.

With right side facing, rejoin MS
yarn to remaining sts, K22[24,24,26],
turn and leave remaining sts on a
spare needle.
K 2 rows.
Continue in MS and garter stitch,
dec 1 st at each end of next and
every alt row until 2 sts remain. K2
tog and fasten off.

With right side facing, rejoin
appropriate colour yarn to remaining
11[11,12,12] sts, K to last 2 sts, K2
tog.
Next row – P to last 2 sts, K2.
Next row – K to last 2 sts, K2 tog.
Rep last 2 rows until 2 sts remain.
Next row – K2.
K2 tog and fasten off.

SLEEVES

With No. 3¼mm needles and MS, cast on 2 sts.
1st row – K2.
2nd row – Inc in 1st st, inc in 2nd st.
3rd row – K4.
Continue in garter st, inc 1 st at each end of next and every alt row until there are 22[22,24,24] sts.
K 2 rows.
Cast on 11[12,12,13] sts at end of next 2 rows. *44[46,48,50] sts.*
K 5 rows, inc 4 sts evenly on last row 48[50,52,54] sts.

Change to No. 4mm needles, work in stripe patt as for Back and **shape sides** by inc 1 st at each end of 3rd and every 6th row until there are 56[58,60,62] sts.
Work a few rows straight until sleeve seam measures approx 13cm, ending with same row of stripe patt as on Back and Front to underarm.

Shape top by casting off 3 sts at beg of next 2 rows, then dec 1 st at each end of next and every following 4th row until 38[38,40,42] sts remain.
Work 1 row.
Now dec 1 st at each end of next and every alt row until 4 sts remain, and ending with a P row. With MS, K 2 rows, then cast off knitways.

TO MAKE UP

Do not press.
Join raglan, side and sleeve seams, matching stripes. Turn sleeve points up and front neck point down; sew button to each point as in photograph.

HAT

With No. 3¼mm needles and MS, cast on 92 sts and K 5 rows; inc 4 sts evenly on last row. *96 sts.*

Change to No. 4mm needles and work in stripe patt for 18 rows, ending with a P row in C.
Break off C.
Continue in MS only; starting with a P row work in stocking stitch until hat measures 10cm from last row of C, ending with a P row.

Shape crown as follows:
Next row – (K10, K2 tog) 8 times.
Next row – P.
Next row – (K9, K2 tog) 8 times.
Next row – P.
Next row – (K8, K2 tog) 8 times.
Next row – P.
Continue thus until the 16 sts remain, ending with a P row.
Next row – K2 tog 8 times.
Break yarn, thread through remaining sts, draw up firmly and fasten off securely.

TO MAKE UP

Do not press.
Join back seam. Fold striped brim to outside. Make a small pom pon using MS and C together and sew to top of hat.

MATERIALS

Pair each No. 3¼mm and No. 4mm needles.

TENSION

On No. 4mm needles, 22 sts and 30 rows to 10cm over stocking stitch.

ABBREVIATIONS

K knit; **P** purl; **sts** stitches; **tog** together; **dec** decrease; **inc** increase; **tbl** through back of loops; **M1** make a stitch by picking up horizontal loop lying before next stitch and working into back of it; **beg** beginning; **rep** repeat; **alt** alternate; **cm** centimetres; **in** inches; **mm** millimetres; **MS** main shade; **C** contrast.

BACK

With No. 3¼mm needles and MS, cast on 100[106,112,118,124] sts and work in K1, P1 rib for 7cm.
Next row – Rib 8[7,7,10,9], (M1, rib 12[13,14,14,15]) 7 times, M1, rib to end. *108[114,120,126,132] sts.*

Change to No. 4mm needles, break off MS, join in C; starting with a K row, work 8 rows stocking stitch.
Break off C, join in MS and work 2 rows stocking stitch.
Break off MS, join in C and work 8 rows stocking stitch.
Break off C, join in MS and continue in stocking stitch until Back measures 54cm, ending with a P row. ****.**

Shape armholes by casting off 3 sts at beg of next 2 rows, then dec 1 st at each end of following 7[7,7,9,9] rows. Work 1 row.
Now dec 1 st at each end of next and

ROBIN

HIS AND HERS
SWEATER WITH
STRIPE DETAIL

*A perfect partnership
with your number-
one batsman.*

1 9 2 0

To fit bust/chest

cm	91	97	102	107	112
in	36	38	40	42	44

Garment measures

cm	98	103	109	114	120
in	38½	40½	43	45	47

Length from top of shoulders

cm	77	78	79	80	81
in	30½	30½	31	31½	32

Sleeve seam

cm	46	46	47	47	47
in	18	18	18½	18½	18½

Patons Moorland Shetland DK

Main shade					
50g balls		10	10	11	11	12
Contrast					
50g balls			1	1	1	1	2

following 1[2,4,3,5] alt rows. *84[88,90,94,96] sts.*
Work straight until Back measures 77[78,79,80,81]cm, ending with a P row.

Shape shoulders by casting off 8[9,9,9,9] sts at beg of next 2 rows, then 8[8,8,9,9] sts at beg of following 4 rows.
Leave remaining 36[38,40,40,42] sts on a spare needle.

FRONT

Work as for Back to ******.

Shape armhole and divide for neck as follows:

1st row – Cast off 3 sts, K48[51,54,57,60] (including st on needle after cast off), K2 tog, turn and leave remaining sts on a spare needle.

Continue on these 49[52,55,58,61] sts for first side as follows:

2nd row – P.
3rd row – K2 tog, K to last 2 sts, K2 tog.
4th row – P to last 2 sts, P2 tog.
5th and 6th rows – As 3rd and 4th.
7th row – K2 tog, K to end.
8th row – P to last 2 sts, P2 tog.
9th row – K2 tog, K to last 2 sts, K2 tog.

1st, 2nd and 3rd sizes

10th row – P.

4th and 5th sizes

10th row – As 8th.

All sizes

11th row – K2 tog, K to end.

12th row – P.
13th row – K2 tog, K to last 2 sts, K2 tog.
14th row – P.
Rep 11th to 14th rows 0[0,1,1,2] times, then rep 11th row 0[1,1,1,1] time. *36[38,38,40,40] sts.*
Keeping armhole edge straight continue dec 1 st at neck edge on every 4th row from previous decrease until 24[25,25,27,27] sts remain.
Work a few rows straight until Front matches Back to shoulder, ending with a P row.

Shape shoulder by casting off 8[9,9,9,9] sts at beg of next row, and 8[8,8,9,9] sts at beg of following 2 alt rows.
With right side facing, leave 2 centre sts on a safety-pin, rejoin yarn to remaining sts, K2 tog, K to end.
2nd row – Cast off 3 sts, P to end.
Complete to correspond with first side, reversing shapings.

SLEEVES

With No. 3¼mm needles and MS, cast on 50[52,52,54,56] sts and work in K1, P1 rib for 9cm.
Next row – Rib 7, (M1, rib 12[13,13,13,14]) 3 times, M1, rib to end. *54[56,56,58,60] sts.*

Change to No. 4mm needles; starting with a K row, work in stocking stitch, **shaping sides** by inc 1 st at each end of 3rd[3rd,9th,9th,9th] and every following 8th[8th,7th,7th,7th] row until there are 80[82,84,86,88] sts. Work straight until sleeve seam measures 46[46,47,47,47]cm, ending with a P row.

Shape top by casting off 3 sts at beg of next 2 rows, then dec 1 st at each end of next row. Work 1[3,3,3,3] rows.

4th and 5th sizes only

Rep last 4 rows once more.

All sizes

Now dec 1 st at each end of next and every alt row until 22 sts remain. Cast off.

TO MAKE UP

With wrong side of work facing, block each piece by pinning out round edges and, omitting ribbing, press lightly, following instructions on yarn labels.
Join right shoulder seam.

With right side facing, No. 3¼mm needles and C, knit up 52[54,56,60,62] sts down left side of neck, K 2 sts from safety-pin (mark these 2 sts with a coloured thread), knit up 52[54,56,60,62] sts up right side of neck, then K36[38,40,40,42] sts from back. *142[148,154,162,168] sts.*
1st row – *K1, P1; rep from * to within 2 sts of marked sts, K2 tog tbl, P2, K2 tog, *P1, K1; rep from * to end.
2nd row – P1, *K1, P1; rep from * to within 2 sts of marked sts, K2 tog tbl, K2, K2 tog, P1, *K1, P1; rep from * to end.
Rep last 2 rows twice more, then 1st row again.
Break off C, join in MS.
Next row – K to within 2 sts of marked sts, K2 tog tbl, K2, K2 tog, K to end.
Next row – As 1st row.
Break off MS, join in C.
Next row – K to within 2 sts of marked sts, K2 tog tbl, K2, K2 tog, K to end.
Now rep 1st and 2nd rows twice.
Cast off evenly in rib, still dec either side of marked sts.
Join neckband, left shoulder, side and sleeve seams. Insert sleeves. Press seams.

MATERIALS

Pair each No. 3¼mm and No. 4mm needles.
10 buttons.
2 shoulder pads.

TENSION

On No. 4mm needles, 19 sts and 30 rows to 10cm over stocking stitch.

ABBREVIATIONS

K knit; **P** purl; **st** stitch; **inc** increase; **dec** decrease; **tog** together; **tbl** through back of loops; **M1** make a stitch by picking up horizontal loop lying before next stitch and working into back of it; **rep** repeat; **beg** beginning; **alt** alternate; **cm** centimetres; **in** inches; **mm** millimetres; **sl** slip; **psso** pass slipped stitch over.

BACK

With No. 3¼mm needles, cast on 68[72,78,84,88] sts and work in K1, P1 rib for 7cm.
Next row – Rib 2[4,3,6,3], (M1 rib 7[7,8,8,9]) 9 times, M1, rib to end. *78[82,88,94,98] sts.*

Change to No. 4mm needles and, starting with a K row, work in stocking stitch until Back measures 31cm, ending with a P row.

Shape armholes by casting off 3 sts at beg of next 2 rows, then dec 1 st at each end of next 3[3,5,7,7] rows. Work 1 row.
Now dec 1 st at each end of next and following 1[2,2,2,3] alt rows. *62[64,66,68,70] sts.*
Work straight until Back measures 49[50,51,52,53]cm, ending with a P row.

Shape shoulders by casting off

DAISY

WOMAN'S SHORT-SLEEVED BUTTONTHROUGH SWEATER

Neat and pretty in textured cotton, Daisy is simple to knit, for all sorts of summer pastimes . . .

1 9 3 6

To fit bust					
cm	81	86	91	97	102
in	32	34	36	38	40

Garment measures					
cm	84	89	94	100	105
in	33	35	37	39½	41½

Length from top of shoulders					
cm	49	50	51	52	53
in	19½	19½	20	20½	21

Sleeve seam					
cm	15	15	15	15	15
in	6	6	6	6	6

Patons Cotton Sahara

50g balls	6	7	7	8	8

6[6,7,7,7] sts at beg of next 2 rows, then 6 sts at beg of following 4 rows. Cast off remaining 26[28,28,30,32] sts.

LEFT FRONT

With No. 3¼mm needles, cast on 34[36,39,42,44] sts and work in K1, P1 rib for 7cm.
Next row – Rib 3[4,4,5,4], (M1, rib 7[7,6,8,9]) 4 times, M1, rib to end. *39[41,44,47,49] sts.*

Change to No. 4mm needles and, starting with a K row, work in stocking stitch until Front measures 31cm, ending with a P row.

Shape armhole by casting off 3 sts at beg of next row. Work 1 row.
Now dec 1 st at armhole edge on next 3[3,5,7,7] rows. Work 1 row.
Now dec 1 st at armhole edge on next and following 1[2,2,2,3] alt rows. *31[32,33,34,35] sts.*
Work straight until Front measures 43[44,45,46,47]cm, ending with a K row.

Shape neck by casting off 5[6,6,7,8] sts at beg of next row, then dec 1 st at neck edge on next 5 rows.
Work 1 row.
Now dec 1 st at neck edge on next and following 2 alt rows. *18[18,19,19,19] sts.*
Work a few rows straight, if required, until Front matches Back to shoulder, ending with a P row.

Shape shoulder by casting off 6[6,7,7,7] sts at beg of next row, then 6 sts at beg of following 2 alt rows.

RIGHT FRONT

Work as for Left Front, reversing all shapings.

SLEEVES

With No. 3¼mm needles, cast on 42[44,46,48,50] sts and work in K1, P1 rib for 2cm.
Next row – Rib 6[5,6,6,7], (M1, rib 10[11,11,12,12]) 3 times, M1, rib to end. *46[48,50,52,54] sts.*

Change to No. 4mm needles and, starting with a K row, work in stocking stitch, shaping sides by inc 1 st at each end of 5th and every following 6th row until there are 56[58,60,62,64] sts.
Work straight until sleeve seam measures 15cm, ending with a P row.

Shape top by casting off 3 sts at beg of next 2 rows, then dec 1 st at each end of next and every following 4th row until 42[44,44,46,46] sts remain.
Work 1 row.
Now dec 1 st at each end of next and every alt row until 18 sts remain.
Cast off.

POCKET FLAP

With No. 3¼mm needles, cast on 19 sts and work as follows:
1st row (right side) – K.
2nd row – K2, P to last 2 sts, K2.

3rd row – K2, K2 tog tbl, K to last 4 sts, K2 tog, K2.
Rep 2nd and 3rd rows until 7 sts remain.

Next row – K2, P3, K2.
Next row – K2, sl 1, K2 tog, psso, K2.

Next row – K2, P1, K2.
Next row – K1, sl 1, K2 tog, psso, K1.
Next row – K3 tog and fasten off.

COLLAR

With No. 3¼mm needles, cast on 71[75,75,79,83] sts and work as follows:
1st row (right side) – K2, *P1, K1; rep from * to last st, K1.
2nd row – K1, *P1, K1; rep from * to end.
Next row – Rib to last 10 sts, turn.
Next row – sl 1, rib to last 10 sts, turn.
Next 2 rows – sl 1, rib to last 16 sts, turn.
Next 2 rows – sl 1, rib to last 22 sts, turn.
Next 2 rows – sl 1, rib to last 28 sts, turn.
Next row – sl 1, rib to end.
Next row – K1, *P1, K1; rep from * to end.
Next row – K2, M1, rib to last 2 sts, M1, K2.
Next row – K1, P2, *K1, P1; rep from * to last 2 sts, P1, K1.
Next row – K2, M1, rib to last 2 sts, M1, K2.
Rep last 4 rows until Collar measures 13cm at centre back.
Cast off loosely in rib.

TO MAKE UP

Do not press.
Join shoulder, side and sleeve seams.
Insert sleeves.

LEFT FRONT BORDER

With No. 3¼mm needles, cast on 9 sts and work as follows:
1st row (right side) – K2, (P1, K1) 3 times, K1.

2nd row – K1, (P1, K1) 4 times.
Rep last 2 rows until border, when slightly stretched, fits up left front to neck; sew in position as you go along. Cast off.

RIGHT FRONT BORDER

Work as for left front border with the addition of 8 buttonholes, the first to come 1cm above lower edge, the last 1cm below top of neck and the remainder spaced evenly between.
First mark position of buttons on left front border with pins to ensure even spacing, then work holes to correspond.

To make a buttonhole: 1st row (right side) – Rib 4, cast off 2, rib to end; 2nd row – Rib, casting on 2 sts over those cast off.
Sew cast-on edge of collar to neck edge, placing collar edges to centre of front borders.

Sew cast-on edge of pocket flap to left front as in photograph. Sew a button to pocket flap (sewing through left front also) just above point, as in photograph. Sew buttons to left front border to correspond with buttonholes.
Sew in shoulder pads.

LEONORA

WOMAN'S V-NECK
SWEATER WITH
CHEVRON-
PATTERNED
FRONT AND
MOCK BELT

*Triumphs on the
lacrosse field,
midnight feasts –
a whole era in one
enchanting jumper.*

1 9 2 4

To fit bust				
cm	86	91	97	102
in	34	36	38	40
Approximate length from top of shoulders				
cm	58	59	60	61
in	23	23½	24	24
Sleeve seam				
cm	44	44	44	44
in	17½	17½	17½	17½

Patons Clansman 4 ply

Main shade (A)				
50g balls		6	6	6	7
1st contrast (B)				
50g balls		2	2	2	2
2nd contrast (C)				
50g balls	1	1	1	1
3rd contrast (D)				
50g balls	1	1	1	1

MATERIALS

Pair each No. 2¾mm and
No. 3¼mm needles.
1 button.

TENSION

On No. 3¼mm needles, 28 sts and
36 rows to 10cm over stocking stitch.

ABBREVIATIONS

K knit; **P** purl; **st** stitch; **tog** together;
tbl through back of loops;
inc increase; **dec** decrease;
beg beginning; **alt** alternate;
rep repeat; **mm** millimetres;
cm centimetres; **in** inches; **A** main
shade; **B** 1st contrast; **C** 2nd contrast;
D 3rd contrast.

NOTE

When working colour pattern on
front, do not carry yarns across back
of work. Divide into separate balls
for each colour section, and twist
yarns on wrong side when changing
colour, to avoid a hole.

BACK

With 2¾mm needles and A, cast on
121[127,135,143] sts and work in rib
as follows:
1st row (right side) – K1, *P1, K1;
rep from * to end.
2nd row – P1, *K1, P1; rep from *
to end.
Rep last 2 rows until work measures
15cm, ending with a 2nd row. Break
off A. ****.**
Join in B and work a further 16 rows
rib in B. Break off B.
Join in A, change to No. 3¼mm
needles and, starting with a K row,
work in stocking stitch for 78 rows.

Continue in stocking stitch and
shape armholes by casting off 3 sts
at beg of next 2 rows, then dec 1 st
at each end of next 7[7,9,9] rows.
Work 1 row.
Now dec 1 st at each end of next and
every alt row until 91[95,99,103] sts
remain. Work 32[34,36,36] rows
straight.

Divide for back opening as
follows:
1st row – K45[47,49,51], turn and
leave remaining sts on a spare
needle.
2nd row – K2, P to end.
3rd row – K.
Rep last 2 rows 4 times more, then
2nd row again.

Continue thus, **shaping shoulder**
by casting off 8[9,10,9] sts at beg of
next row, then 9[9,9,10] sts at beg of
following 2 alt rows.
Cast off remaining 19[20,21,22] sts.

Rejoin yarn to remaining sts, cast off
1, K to end.
Finish to match first side.

FRONT

Work as for Back to ****.**
Joining in and breaking off colours as
required, work as follows:
1st and 2nd rows – Rib
51[54,58,62] B, 19 A, 51[54,58,62] B.
3rd to 6th rows – Rib 51[54,58,62]
B, 2 A, 15 B, 2 A, 51[54,58,62] B.
7th to 10th rows – Rib 51[54,58,62]
B, 2 A, 15 C, 2 A, 51[54,58,62] B.
11th to 14th rows – Rib
51[54,58,62] B, 2 A, 15 D, 2 A,
51[54,58,62] B.
15th and 16th rows – As 1st and
2nd.

Change to No. 3¼mm needles,
join in A and, starting with a K row,
work in stocking stitch for 14 rows.
Work colour V pattern as follows:
1st row – K59[62,66,70] A, 3 B,
59[62,66,70] A.
2nd row – P59[62,66,70] A, 3 B,
59[62,66,70] A.
3rd row – As 1st.
4th row – P58[61,65,69] A, 5 B,
58[61,65,69] A.
5th row – K58[61,65,69] A, 5 B,
58[61,65,69] A.

6th row – As 4th.
7th row – K57[60,64,68] A, 7 B,
57[60,64,68] A.
8th row – P57[60,64,68] A, 7 B,
57[60,64,68] A.
9th row – As 7th.
Continue thus, moving 1 st over on
every 3rd row until you have
completed the 3 rows with 27 sts in
B, ending with a K row.

Continue as follows:
1st row – P46[49,53,57] A, 14 B, 1
C, 14 B, 46[49,53,57] A.
2nd row – K46[49,53,57] A, 14 B, 1
C, 14 B, 46[49,53,57] A.
3rd row – As 1st.
4th row – K45[48,52,56] A, 14 B, 3
C, 14 B, 45[48,52,56] A.
5th row – P45[48,52,56] A, 14 B, 3
C, 14 B, 45[48,52,56] A.

6th row – As 4th.
7th row – P44[47,51,55] A, 14 B, 5
C, 14 B, 44[47,51,55] A.
8th row – K44[47,51,55] A, 14 B, 5
C, 14 B, 44[47,51,55] A.
9th row – As 7th.

10th row – K43[46,50,54] A, 14 B, 7
C, 14 B, 43[46,50,54] A.
11th row – P43[46,50,54] A, 14 B, 7
C, 14 B, 43[46,50,54] A.
12th row – As 10th.
13th row – P42[45,49,53] A, 14 B, 4
C, 1 D, 4 C, 14 B, 42[45,49,53] A.
14th row – K42[45,49,53] A, 14 B, 4
C, 1 D, 4 C, 14 B, 42[45,49,53] A.

15th row – As 13th.
16th row – K41[44,48,52] A, 14 B, 4
C, 3 D, 4 C, 14 B, 41[44,48,52] A.
17th row – P41[44,48,52] A, 14 B, 4
C, 3 D, 4 C, 14 B, 41[44,48,52] A.
18th row – As 16th.
19th row – P40[43,47,51] A, 14 B, 4
C, 5 D, 4 C, 14 B, 40[43,47,51] A.
20th row – K40[43,47,51] A, 14 B, 4
C, 5 D, 4 C, 14 B, 40[43,47,51] A.

21st row – As 19th.
22nd row – K39[42,46,50] A, 14 B,
4 C, 7 D, 4 C, 14 B, 39[42,46,50] A.
23rd row – P39[42,46,50] A, 14 B, 4
C, 7 D, 4 C, 14 B, 39[42,46,50] A.
24th row – As 22nd.

25th row – P38[41,45,49] A, 14 B, 4
C, 9 D, 4 C, 14 B, 38[41,45,49] A.

Shape armholes as follows:
26th row – Cast off 3, K35[38,42,46]
A (including st on needle after cast
off), 14 B, 4 C, 9 D, 4 C, 14 B,
38[41,45,49] A.
27th row – Cast off 3, P35[38,42,46]
A (including st on needle after cast
off), 14 B, 4 C, 9 D, 4 C, 14 B,
35[38,42,46] A.
28th row – K2 tog A, K32[35,39,43]
A, 14 B, 4 C, 5 D, P1 D, K5 D, 4 C,
14 B, 32[35,39,43] A, K2 tog A.
29th row – P2 tog A, P31[34,38,42]
A, 14 B, 4 C, 5 D, K1 D, P5 D, 4 C,
14 B, 31[34,38,42] A, P2 tog A.
30th row – K2 tog A, K30[33,37,41]
A, 14 B, 4 C, 5 D, P1 D, K5 D, 4 C,
14 B, 30[33,37,41] A, K2 tog A.

31st row – P2 tog A, P28[31,35,39]
A, 14 B, 4 C, 6 D, K1 D, P6 D, 4 C,
14 B, 28[31,35,39] A, P2 tog A.
32nd row – K2 tog A, K27[30,34,38]
A, 14 B, 4 C, 4 D, (P1, K1) 3 times
in D, K3 D, 4 C, 14 B, 27[30,34,38]
A, K2 tog A.
33rd row – P2 tog A, P26[29,33,37]
A, 14 B, 4 C, 4 D, (K1 P1) 3 times in
D, P3 D, 4 C, 14 B, 26[29,33,37] A,
P2 tog A.
34th row – K2 tog A, K24[27,31,35]
A, 14 B, 4 C, 5 D, (P1, K1) 3 times
in D, K4 D, 4 C, 14 B, 24[27,31,35]
A, K2 tog A.
35th row – P2 tog A 0[0,1,1] time,
P25[28,30,34] A, 14 B, 4 C, 5 D,
(K1, P1) 3 times in D, P4 D, 4 C, 14
B, 25[28,30,34] A, P2 tog A 0[0,1,1]
time.

36th row – K2 tog A, K23[26,29,33]
A, 14 B, 4 C, 3 D, (P1, K1) 5 times
in D, K2 D, 4 C, 14 B, 23[26,29,33]
A, K2 tog A.

37th row – P23[26,29,33] A, 14 B, 4 C, 4 D, (K1, P1) 5 times in D, P3 D, 4 C, 14 B, 23[26,29,33] A.

38th row – K2 tog A, K21[24,27,31] A, 14 B, 4 C, 4 D, (P1, K1) 5 times in D, K3 D, 4 C, 14 B, 21[24,27,31] A, K2 tog A.

39th row – P22[25,28,32] A, 14 B, 4 C, 4 D, (K1, P1) 5 times in D, P3 D, 4 C, 14 B, 22[25,28,32] A.

Divide for neck as follows:

40th row – K2 tog A, K19[22,25,29] A, 14 B, 4 C, 4 D, (P1, K1) twice in D, K1 D, turn, and leave remaining sts on a spare needle.

41st row – (K1, P1) 3 times in D, P3 D, 4 C, 14 B, P to end in A.

42nd row – K2 tog A, K18[21,24,28] A, 14 B, 4 C, 4 D, (P1, K1) twice in D, K1 D.

43rd row – (K1, P1) twice in D, K1 D, P2 tog D, P3 D, 4 C, 14 B, P to end in A.

44th row – K2 tog A, K16[19,22,26] A, 14 B, 4 C, 4 D, (P1, K1) twice in D, K1 D.

45th row – As 41st.

46th row – K2 tog A 0[1,1,1] time, K16[17,20,24] A, 14 B, 4 C, 3 D, K2 tog D, (P1, K1) twice in D, K1 D.

47th row – As 41st.

48th row – K2 tog A 0[0,1,1] time, K16[18,19,23] A, 14 B, 4 C, 4 D, (P1, K1) twice in D, K1 D.

49th row – (K1, P1) twice in D, K1 D, P2 tog D, P3 D, 4 C, 14 B, P to end in A.

50th row – K2 tog A 0[0,0,1] time, K15[17,19,21] A, 14 B, 4 C, 4 D, (P1, K1) twice in D, K1 D.

51st row – As 41st.

52nd row – K2 tog A 0[0,0,1] time, K14[16,18,19] A, 14 B, 4 C, 3 D, K2 tog D, (P1, K1) twice in D, K1 D.

53rd row – As 41st.

54th row – K14[16,18,20] A, 14 B, 4 C, 4 D, (P1, K1) twice in D, K1 D.

55th row – (K1, P1) twice in D, K1 D, P2 tog D, P3 D, 4 C, 1 B, P2 tog B, P11 B, P to end in A.

56th row – K13[15,17,19] A, 13 B, 4 C, 4 D, (P1, K1) twice in D, K1 D.

57th row – (K1, P1) 3 times in D, P3 D, 4 C, 13 B, P to end in A.

58th row – K12[14,16,18] A, 13 B, 4 C, 3 D, K2 tog D, (P1, K1) twice in D, K1 D.

59th row – As 57th.

60th row – K12[14,16,18] A, 13 B, 4 C, 4 D, (P1, K1) twice in D, K1 D.

61st row – (K1, P1) twice in D, K1 D, P2 tog D, P3 D, 4 C, 13 B, P to end in A.

62nd row – K11[13,15,17] A, 13 B, 4 C, 4 D, (P1, K1) twice in D, K1 D.

63rd row – As 57th.

64th row – K10[12,14,16] A, 13 B, 4 C, 3 D, K2 tog D, (P1, K1) twice in D, K1 D.

65th row – As 57th.

66th row – K10[12,14,16] A, 13 B, 4

C, 4 D, (P1, K1) twice in D, K1 D.
67th row – (K1, P1) twice in D, K1 D, P2 tog D, P3 D, P4 C, P1 B, P2 tog B, P10 B, P to end in A.
68th row – K9[11,13,15] A, 12 B, 4 C, 4 D, (P1, K1) twice in D, K1 D.
69th row – (K1, P1) twice in D, K1 D, P4 D, 4 C, 12 B, P to end in A.

70th row – K8[10,12,14] A, 12 B, 4 C, 3 D, K2 tog D, (P1, K1) twice in D, K1 D.
71st row – As 69th.
72nd row – K8[10,12,14] A, 12 B, 4 C, 4 D, (P1, K1) twice in D, K1 D.
73rd row – (K1, P1) twice in D, K1 D, P2 tog D, P3 D, 4 C, 12 B, P to end in A.
74th row – K7[9,11,13] A, 12 B, 4 C, 4 D, (P1, K1) twice in D, K1 D.
75th row – As 69th.

76th row – K6[8,10,12] A, 12 B, 4 C, 3 D, K2 tog D, (P1, K1) twice in D, K1 D.
77th row – As 69th.
78th row – K6[8,10,12] A, 12 B, 4 C, 4 D, (P1, K1) twice in D, K1 D.
79th row – (K1, P1) twice in D, K1 D, P2 tog D, P3 D, 4 C, 1 B, P2 tog B, P9 B, P to end in A.

80th row – K5[7,9,11] A, 11 B, 4 C, 4 D, (P1, K1) twice in D, K1 D.
81st row – (K1, P1) twice in D, K1 D, P4 D, 4 C, 11 B, P to end in A.
82nd row – K4[6,8,10] A, 11 B, 4 C, 3 D, K2 tog D, (P1, K1) twice in D, K1 D.
83rd row – As 81st.
84th row – K4[6,8,10] A, 11 B, 4 C, 4 D, (P1, K1) twice in D, K1 D.

85th row – (K1, P1) twice in D, K1 D, P2 tog D, P3 D, 4 C, 11 B, P to end in A.
86th row – K3[5,7,9] A, 11 B, 4 C, 4 D, (P1, K1) twice in D, K1 D.

87th row – As 81st.
88th row – K2[4,6,8] A, 11 B, 4 C, 3 D, K2 tog D, (P1, K1) twice in D, K1 D.
89th row – As 81st.

2nd, 3rd and 4th sizes only

90th row – K4[6,8] A, 11 B, 4 C, 4 D, (P1, K1) twice in D, K1 D.
91st row – (K1, P1) twice in D, K1 D, P2 tog D, P3 D, 4 C, 11 B, P to end in D.
92nd row – K3[5,7] A, 11 B, 4 C, 4 D, (P1, K1) twice in D, K1 D.
93rd row – As 81st.

3rd and 4th sizes only

94th row – K4[6] A, 11 B, 4 C, 3 D, K2 tog D, (P1, K1) twice in D, K1 D.
95th row – As 81st.
96th row – K4[6] A, 11 B, 4 C, 4 D, (P1, K1) twice in D, K1 D.
97th row – (K1, P1) twice in D, K1 D, (P2 tog D) 0[1] time, P4[3] D, 4 C, 11 B, P to end in A.

4th size only

98th row – K5 A, 11 B, 4 C, 4 D, (P1, K1) twice in D, K1 D.
99th row – As 81st.
100th row – K4 A, 11 B, 4 C, 5 D, (P1, K1) twice in D, K1 D.
101st row – (K1, P1) twice in D, K1 D, P5 D, 4 C, 11 B, 4 A.

All sizes

Keeping colours as set, **shape shoulder** by casting off 8[9,10,9] sts at beg of next row.
Work 1 row.
Now cast off 9[9,9,10] sts at beg of next and following alt row.

With right side facing, rejoin D yarn

to remaining sts, cast off 1 (thus leaving 1 st on right-hand needle), (K1, P1) twice in D, K4 D, 4 C, 14 B, 19[22,25,29] A, K2 tog A.
Complete to match left side, reading rows from 41st row in reverse, and when working dec in D and B yarns, work K2 tog tbl in place of K2 tog; and P2 tog tbl in place of P2 tog.

SLEEVES

With No. 2¾mm needles and A, cast on 54[56,56,58] sts and work in K1, P1 rib for 7cm. Break off A.
Now work 4 rows in rib in B, 4 in C, and 4 in D, inc 6 sts evenly on last row. *60[62,62,64] sts.*
Break off yarns.

Rejoin A, **change to No. 3¼mm needles** and, starting with a K row, work in stocking stitch, shaping sides by inc 1 st at each end of 9th[3rd,next,9th] and every following 9th[9th,8th,7th] row until there are 86[90,94,98] sts.
Work a few rows straight until sleeve seam measures 44cm ending with a P row.

Shape top by casting off 3 sts at beg of next 2 rows, then dec 1 st at each end of every alt row until 36 sts remain.
Cast off.

TO MAKE UP

Omitting ribbing, press parts lightly following instructions on the yarn band.
Join shoulder, side and sleeve seams.
Insert sleeves.
Press seams.
Make a button loop on right top edge of back opening and sew button on to left top edge to correspond.

MATERIALS

Pair each No. 4mm and No. 5½mm needles.
Shoulder pads.

TENSION

On No. 5½mm needles, 15 sts and 20 rows to 10cm over stocking stitch.

ABBREVIATIONS

K knit; **P** purl; **sts** stitches; **tog** together; **dec** decrease; **inc** increase; **M1** make a stitch by picking up horizontal loop lying before next stitch and working into back of it; **patt** pattern; **rep** repeat; **beg** beginning; **alt** alternate; **cm** centimetres; **in** inches; **mm** millimetres; **MS** main shade; **B** 1st contrast; **C** 2nd contrast.

NOTE

When working in stripes, carry yarns loosely up side of work.

BACK

With No. 4mm needles and MS, cast on 60[64,68,72,76] sts and work in K1, P1 rib for 5cm.
Next row – Rib 2[4,6,6,5], (M1, rib 5[5,5,6,6]) 11 times, M1, rib to end. *72[76,80,84,88] sts.*
Break off MS.

Change to No. 5½mm needles.
Joining in colours as required and carrying yarn up side of work when not in use, start with a K row and work in stocking stitch and stripe patt as follows:
1st to 5th rows – In B.
6th to 8th rows – In MS.
9th and 10th rows – In C.
11th to 15th rows – In MS.
16th to 18th rows – In B.

B E T H

WOMAN'S STRIPED MOHAIR SWEATER

There's no limit to the wonderful colour contrasts that wait to be knitted into this gorgeous sweater.

1 9 2 4

To fit bust					
cm	81	86	91	97	102
in	32	34	36	38	40
Garment measures					
cm	94	99	104	109	114
in	37	39	41	43	45
Length from top of shoulders					
cm	62	63	64	65	66
in	24½	25	25	25½	26
Sleeve, measured down centre					
cm	44	44	44	44	44
in	17½	17½	17½	17½	17½

Patons Mohair Focus

Main shade (MS)					
25g balls		6	6	7	8	8
1st contrast (B)					
25g balls		5	5	6	6	7
2nd contrast (C)					
25g balls		3	3	3	3	3

19th and 20th rows – In C.
These 20 rows form stripe patt.
Continue in patt until Back measures 43cm, ending with a P row.
Continue in stripe patt and **shape armholes** by casting off 3 sts at beg of next 2 rows, then dec 1 st at each end of next 5[5,7,7,7] rows. Work 1 row.
Now dec 1 st at each end of next and following 1[2,1,2,3] alt rows. *52[54,56,58,60] sts. **.*
Continue straight in patt until Back measures 62[63,64,65,66]cm, ending with a P row.

Shape shoulders by casting off 5[5,6,6,5] sts at beg of next 2 rows, then 5[5,5,5,6] sts at beg of following 4 rows. Leave remaining 22[24,24,26,26] sts on a spare needle.

FRONT

Work as for Back to **.
Work a few rows straight, if required, until Front measures 49[50,51,51,52]cm, ending with a P row.

Keeping stripe patt correct, **divide for neck** as follows:
Next row – K24[25,26,27,28], K2 tog, turn and leave remaining sts on a spare needle.
Continue on these 25[26,27,28,29] sts for first side and dec 1 st at neck edge on every alt row until 15[15,16,16,17] sts remain.
Work a few rows straight, if required, until Front matches Back to shoulder, ending with a P row.

Shape shoulder by casting off 5[5,6,6,5] sts at beg of next row, then 5[5,5,5,6] sts at beg of following 2 alt rows.
With right side facing, rejoin

appropriate colour yarn to remaining sts, K2 tog, K to end.
Finish to correspond with first side, reversing shapings.

SLEEVES

With No. 4mm needles and MS, cast on 28[30,30,32,32] sts and work in K1, P1 rib for 6cm.
Next row – Rib 3[4,4,4,4], (M1, rib 7[7,7,8,8]) 3 times, M1, rib to end. *32[34,34,36,36] sts.*

Change to No. 5½mm needles and, starting with a K row, work in stocking stitch and stripe patt as for Back, shaping sides by inc 1 st at each end of 9th[9th,3rd,3rd,3rd] and every following 9th[9th,8th,8th,8th] row until there are 46[48,50,52,52] sts.
Work a few rows in stripe patt until sleeve, when measured down centre, measures approx 44cm, ending with same stripe row as at armhole on Back and Front.

Continue in stripe patt and **shape top** by casting off 3 sts at beg of next 2 rows, then dec 1 st at each end of following row. Work 1[1,1,1,3] rows.
Dec 1 st at each end of next and every alt row, until 14 sts remain. Cast off.

TO MAKE UP

Do not press.
Join shoulder seams.

LEFT COLLAR

With wrong side facing, No. 4mm needles and MS, knit up 32[32,32,34,34] sts up right side of neck, then K11[12,12,13,13] sts from half of back, inc 2[3,3,2,2] sts evenly. *45[47,47,49,49] sts.*
1st row (wrong side) – K1, *P1, K1; rep from * to end.
2nd row – K2, *P1, K1; rep from * to last st, P1.
Next 2 rows – Rib 4 turn, slip 1, rib to end.
Next 2 rows – Rib 8 turn, slip 1, rib to end.
Next 2 rows – Rib 12 turn, slip 1, rib to end.
Next 2 rows – Rib 16 turn, slip 1, rib to end.
Next 2 rows – Rib 20 turn, slip 1, rib to end.
Next row – *K1, P1; rep from * to last st, M1, K1.
Next row – K2, M1, *P1, K1; rep from * to last st, P1.
Next row – K1, *P1, K1; rep from * to last 3 sts, P2, K1.
Next row – K2, M1, *K1, P1; rep from * to end.
Rep last 4 rows 4 times more.
Cast off loosely in rib.

RIGHT COLLAR

With wrong side facing, No. 4mm needles and MS, K remaining 11[12,12,13,13] sts from back, inc 2[3,3,2,2] sts evenly, then knit up 32[32,32,34,34] sts down left side of neck. *45[47,47,49,49] sts.*

1st row (wrong side) – K1, *P1, K1; rep from * to end.
Next 2 rows – Rib 4 turn, slip 1, rib to end.
Next 2 rows – Rib 8 turn, slip 1, rib to end.
Next 2 rows – Rib 12 turn, slip 1, rib to end.
Next 2 rows – Rib 16 turn, slip 1, rib to end.
Next 2 rows – Rib 20 turn, slip 1, rib to end.

Next row – P1, *K1, P1; rep from * to last 2 sts, K2.
Next row – *K1, P1; rep from * to last st, K1.
Next row – *P1, K1; rep from * to last 3 sts, P1, M1, K2.
Next row – K1, P2, *K1, P1; rep from * to last st, K1.
Next row – *P1, K1; rep from * to last 2 sts, M1, K2.
Rep last 4 rows 4 times more.
Cast off loosely in rib.

Join collar at centre back.
Join side and sleeve seams.
Insert sleeves.

MATERIALS

Pair each Nos. 3¼mm and 4mm
needles. 7 buttons.

TENSION

On No. 4mm needles, 26 sts and 26
rows to 10cm, measured over colour
pattern.

ABBREVIATIONS

K knit; **P** purl; **sts** stitches;
inc increase; **dec** decrease;
tog together; **M1** make a stitch by
picking up horizontal loop lying
before next stitch and working into
back of it; **patt** pattern; **rep** repeat;
beg beginning; **alt** alternate;
cm centimetres; **in** inches;
mm millimetres; **MS** main shade.

NOTE

When working in patt from chart,
read odd rows K from right to left
and even rows P from left to right.
Strand yarns loosely across back of
work over not more than 3 sts at a
time to keep fabric elastic. Carry MS
and 1st contrast yarns loosely up side
of work. Join in and break off 2nd
contrast and 3rd contrast as required.

BACK

With No. 3¼mm needles and MS,
cast on 98[104,110,116,122] sts and
work 4cm in K1, P1 rib.
Next row – Rib 9[8,11,10,1], (M1,
rib 4[4,4,4,5])20[22,22,24,24] times,
M1, rib to end. *119
[127,133,141,147] sts.*

Change to No. 4mm needles and
work in patt from chart A (see p.
69). Rep the 16 patt sts 7[7,8,8,9]
times across, working the first
3[7,2,6,1] sts and last 4[8,3,7,2] sts

EDGAR

MAN'S CLASSIC
FAIR ISLE
CARDIGAN

*What a figure a man
cuts on the green
in this striking
Fair Isle design!*

1 9 2 8

To fit chest

cm	91	97	102	107	112
in	36	38	40	42	44

Garment measures

cm	94	100	105	110	115
in	37	39½	41½	43½	45½

Length from top of shoulders

cm	64	65	66	67	68
in	25	25½	26	26½	27

Sleeve seam (approx)

cm	47	47	47	47	47
in	18½	18½	18½	18½	18½

Patons DK

Main shade (MS)					
50g balls		7	8	8	9	9
1st contrast					
50g balls			1	1	1	2	2
2nd contrast					
50g balls			1	1	1	1	2
3rd contrast					
50g balls			2	2	2	2	3

on K rows, and the first 4[8,3,7,2] sts
and last 3[7,2,6,1] sts on P rows as
indicated on the chart.
Continue in patt until Back measures
41cm, ending with right side facing
for next row.

Keeping patt correct, **shape
armholes** by casting off 3 sts at beg
of next 2 rows, then dec 1 st at each
end of next 5[7,7,9,11] rows. Work 1
row.
Now dec 1 st at each end of next and
every alt row until 99
[101,105,107,109] sts remain.
Work straight until Back measures
64[65,66,67,68]cm, ending with right
side facing for next row.

Shape shoulders by casting off 10
[10,9,10,10] sts at beg of next 2
rows, then 9[9,10,10,10] sts at beg of
following 4 rows. Cast off remaining
43[45,47,47,49] sts.

LEFT FRONT

With No. 3¼mm needles and MS,
cast on 48[52,54,58,60] sts and work
4cm in K1, P1 rib.
Next row – Rib 2[4,3,5,4], (M1, rib
4)11[11,12,12,13] times, M1, rib to
end. *60[64,67,71,74] sts.*

Change to No. 4mm needles and
work in patt from chart B (see p.
69). Rep the 16 patt sts 3[3,4,4,4]
times across, working the first
3[7,2,6,1] sts and last 9[9,1,1,9] sts
on K rows, and the first 9[9,1,1,9] sts
and last 3[7,2,6,1] sts on P rows
as indicated on chart B.
Continue in patt until Front matches
Back to armhole, ending with right
side facing for next row.

Keeping patt correct, **shape armhole**
and **front slope** as follows:
1st row – Cast off 3 sts, patt to last

2 sts, K2 tog.

2nd row – Patt to end.

3rd row – K2 tog, patt to last 2 sts, K2 tog.

4th row – Patt to last 2 sts, P2 tog.

Rep 3rd and 4th rows 1[2,2,3,4] times, then 3rd row again.

Now rep 2nd and 3rd rows 2[3,4,5,5] times.

Keeping armhole edge straight, continue dec 1 st at front edge on following 6[5,5,3,3] alt rows.

Now dec 1 st at front edge on every 3rd row from previous dec until 28[28,29,30,30] sts remain.

Work a few rows straight until Front matches Back at shoulder, ending with right side facing for next row.

Shape shoulder by casting off 10[10,9,10,10] sts at beg of next row, and 9[9,10,10,10] sts at beg of following 2 rows.

RIGHT FRONT

Work to correspond with Left Front, reversing all shapings and reversing patt from chart B, reading odd rows K from *left* to *right*, and even rows P from *right* to *left*.

SLEEVES

With No. 3¼mm needles and MS, cast on 48[50,52,54,56] sts and work in K1, P1 rib for 7cm.

Next row – Rib 3[7,5,3,7], (M1, rib 3)14[12,14,16,14] times, M1, rib to end. *63[63,67,71,71] sts.*

Change to No. 4mm needles and place patt as for 2nd[2nd,5th,1st,1st] size on chart A; **shape sides** by inc 1 st at each end of 5th[7th,5th,5th,7th] and every following 6th[5th,6th,6th,5th] row until there are 93[97,99,103,105] sts, taking inc sts into patt.

Work a few rows straight until sleeve seam measures approx 47cm, ending with same patt row as on Back and Fronts at underarm, ending with right side facing for next row.

Keeping patt correct, **shape top** by casting off 3 sts at beg of next 2 rows, then dec 1 st at each end of next and every alt row until 61[61,61,65,61] sts remain.

Now dec 1 st at each end of every row until 25 sts remain. Cast off.

TO MAKE UP

With wrong side of work facing, block each piece by pinning out

round edges and, omitting ribbing, press parts lightly following instructions on yarn labels.

Join shoulder, side and sleeve seams. Insert sleeves.

RIGHT FRONT BORDER

With No. 3¼mm needles and MS, cast on 9 sts and work as follows:

1st row (right side) – K2, (P1, K1) 3 times, K1.

2nd row – (K1, P1) 4 times, K1.

Rep last 2 rows until border, when slightly stretched, fits up right front and round to centre back neck. Cast off and sew neatly in position.

LEFT FRONT BORDER

Work as for right front border with the addition of 7 buttonholes, the first to come 1cm above lower edge, the seventh level with start of front slope shaping and the remainder spaced evenly between.

To make a buttonhole: 1st row (right side) – rib 3, cast off 2, rib to end; 2nd row – rib, casting on 2 sts over those cast off.

Join borders at centre back.

Press seams. Sew on buttons.

KEY

☐ = MS   ◨ = 2ND CONTRAST

◉ = 1ST CONTRAST   ⊡ = 3RD CONTRAST

CHART B

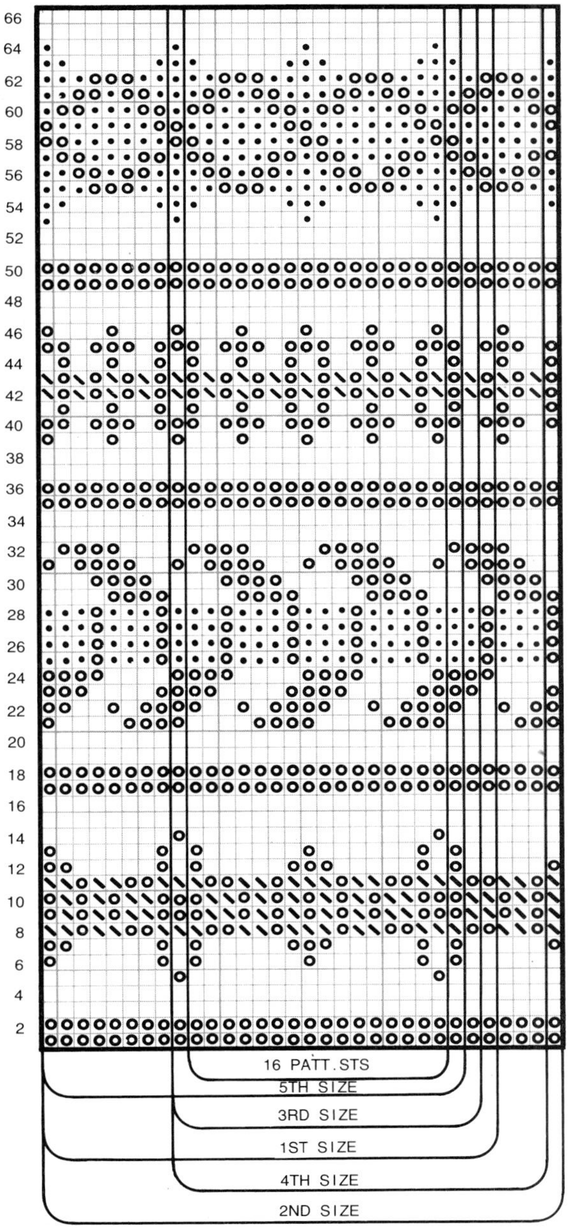

66
64
62
60
58
56
54
52
50
48
46
44
42
40
38
36
34
32
30
28
26
24
22
20
18
16
14
12
10
8
6
4
2

65
63
61
59
57
55
53
51
49
47
45
43
41
39
37
35
33
31
29
27
25
23
21
19
17
15
13
11
9
7
5
3
1

16 PATT. STS
5TH SIZE
3RD SIZE
1ST SIZE
4TH SIZE
2ND SIZE

CHART A

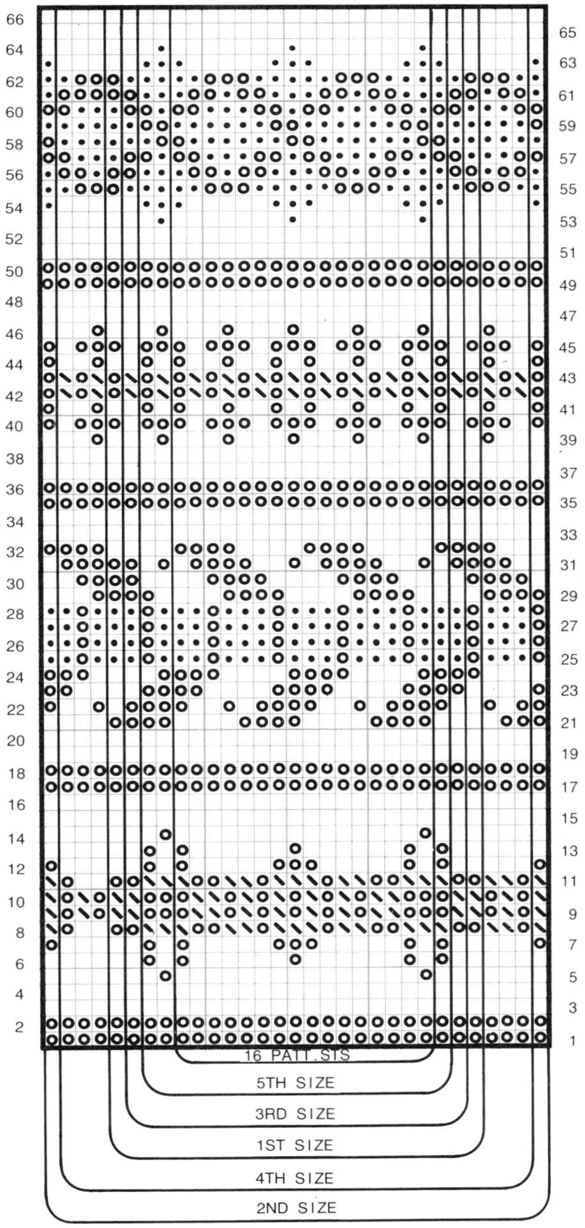

66
64
62
60
58
56
54
52
50
48
46
44
42
40
38
36
34
32
30
28
26
24
22
20
18
16
14
12
10
8
6
4
2

65
63
61
59
57
55
53
51
49
47
45
43
41
39
37
35
33
31
29
27
25
23
21
19
17
15
13
11
9
7
5
3
1

16 PATT. STS
5TH SIZE
3RD SIZE
1ST SIZE
4TH SIZE
2ND SIZE

MATERIALS

Pair each Nos. 3¼mm and No. 4mm needles. Shoulder pads if required.

TENSION

On No. 4mm needles, 26 sts and 28 rows to 10cm over colour pattern.

ABBREVIATIONS

K knit; **P** purl; **sts** stitches; **tog** together; **inc** increase; **dec** decrease; **patt** pattern; **rep** repeat; **beg** beginning; **alt** alternate; **M1** make a stitch by picking up horizontal loop lying before next stitch and working into back of it; **cm** centimetres; **in** inches; **mm** millimetres; **MS** main shade.

NOTE

When working in patt from chart, read odd rows K from right to left and even rows P from left to right. Strand yarns loosely across back of work over not more than 4 sts at a time, to keep fabric elastic.

BACK

With No. 3¼mm needles and MS, cast on 86[92,98,104,110] sts and work in K1, P1 rib for 4cm.
Next row – Rib 5[5,5,8,11], (M1, rib 3)25[27,29,29,29] times, M1, rib to end. *112[120,128,134,140] sts.*

Change to No. 4mm needles and joining in colours as required, work in patt from chart (see p. 72); rep the 16 patt sts 7[7,8,8,8] times across row, working the first 7[3,7,2,5] sts and last 9[5,9,4,7] sts on K rows, and first 9[5,9,4,7] sts and last 7[3,7,2,5] sts on P rows as indicated.
Continue in patt until Back measures 42cm, ending with right side facing for next row.**

A N G E L A

WOMAN'S CLASSIC V-NECK FAIRISLE SWEATER

Subtle colours or bold contrasts – it's up to you.

1 9 3 9

To fit bust

cm	81	86	91	97	102
in	32	34	36	38	40

Garment measures (approx)

cm	86	92	98	103	107
in	34	36	38½	40½	42

Approximate length from top of shoulders

cm	60	61	62	63	64
in	23½	24	24½	25	25

Approximate length of sleeve seam

cm	46	46	46	47	47
in	18	18	18	18½	18½

Patons DK

Main shade					
50g balls	8	9	9	10	10
1st contrast					
50g balls	1	1	1	2	2
2nd contrast					
50g balls	3	3	3	4	4
3rd contrast					
50g balls	1	1	1	1	1

Keeping patt correct, **shape armholes** by casting off 3 sts at beg of next 2 rows, then dec 1 st at each end of following 7[9,9,11,11] rows. Work 1 row.
Now dec 1 st at each end of next and every alt row until 84[88,92,94,98] sts remain.
Work straight until Back measures 60[61,62,63,64]cm, ending with right side facing for next row.

Shape shoulders by casting off 7[8,9,9,8] sts at beg of next 2 rows, then 8[8,8,8,9] sts at beg of following 2 rows.
Leave remaining 38[40,42,44,46] sts on a spare needle.

FRONT

Work as for Back to **.

Keeping patt correct, **shape armhole** and **divide for neck** as follows:
1st row – Cast off 3 sts, patt 51[55,59,62,65] sts (including st on needle after cast off), K2 tog, turn and leave remaining sts on a spare needle.

Continue on these 52[56,60,63,66] sts for first side as follows:
2nd row – In patt.
3rd row – K2 tog, patt to last 2 sts, K2 tog.
4th row – Patt to last 2 sts, P2 tog.
Rep 3rd and 4th rows 2[3,3,4,4] times more, then rep 3rd and 2nd rows 4[4,6,6,7] times, then 3rd row again. *33[34,34,34,35] sts.*
Work 1[1,2,2,2] rows.
Now dec 1 st at neck edge on next and every following 3rd row until 23[24,25,25,26] sts remain.
Work a few rows straight until Front matches Back to shoulder, ending with right side facing for next row.

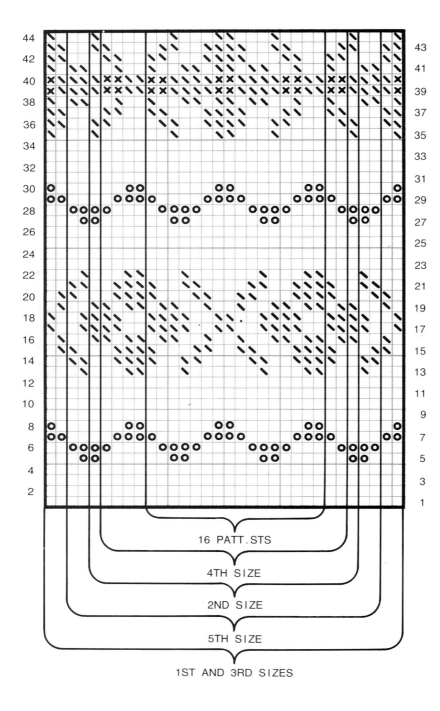

16 PATT.STS

4TH SIZE

2ND SIZE

5TH SIZE

1ST AND 3RD SIZES

Shape shoulder by casting off 7[8,9,9,8] sts at beg of next row, then 8[8,8,8,9] sts at beg of 2 following alt rows.

With right side of work facing, rejoin appropriate colour yarn to remaining sts; K2 tog, patt to end.
Next row – Cast off 3 sts, patt to end.
Finish to correspond with first side, reversing all shapings.

SLEEVES

With No. 3¼mm needles and MS, cast on 42[44,44,46,46] sts and work in K1, P1 rib for 7cm.
Next row – Rib 4[4,5,3,3], (M1, rib 3[4,3,3,3])11[9,11,13,13] times, M1, rib to end. *54[54,56,60,60] sts.*

Change to No. 4mm needles.
Joining in colours as required, work in patt from chart as for 4th[4th,2nd,5th,5th] size, shaping sides by inc 1 st at each end of 9th[5th,9th,9th,5th] row and every following 7th[7th,6th,6th,6th] row until there are 78[80,84,88,90] sts, taking inc sts into patt.
Work straight until sleeve seam measures approx 46[46,46,47,47]cm, ending with same patt row as on Back and Front to armhole.

Keeping patt correct, **shape top** by casting off 3 sts at beg of next 2 rows, then dec 1 st at each end of next and every alt row until 48 [48,48,52,52] sts remain.
Work 1 row.
KEY

☐ = MS

◉ = 1ST CONTRAST

◥ = 2ND CONTRAST

☒ = 3RD CONTRAST

Now dec 1 st at each end of every row until 24 sts remain. Cast off.

TO MAKE UP

With wrong side of work facing, block each piece by pinning out round edges and, omitting ribbing, press lightly following instructions on the yarn label. Join right shoulder seam.

NECKBAND

With right side facing, No. 3¼mm needles and MS, knit up 42[44,46,48,50] sts down left side of neck, 1 st front centre V (mark this st with a coloured thread), 42[44,46,48,50] sts up right side of neck, then K 38[40,42,44,46] sts from back neck. *123 [129,135,141,147] sts.*

Next row – *K1, P1; rep from * to within 2 sts of marked st, K2 tog tbl, P1, K2 tog, *P1, K1; rep from * to end.

Next row – P1, *K1, P1; rep from * to within 2 sts of marked st, K2 tog tbl, K1, K2 tog, P1, *K1, P1; rep from * to end.

Rep last 2 rows twice more.

Cast off evenly in rib, still dec either side of marked st as before.

Join left shoulder, neckband, side and sleeve seams.

Insert sleeves.

Press seams.

Sew in shoulder pads if required.

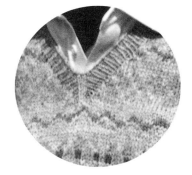

MATERIALS

Pair each No. 3¼mm and No. 4mm needles.

TENSION

On No. 4mm needles, 26 sts and 27 rows to 10cm over colour pattern.

ABBREVIATIONS

K knit; **P** purl; **sts** stitches; **tog** together; **dec** decrease; **patt** pattern; **beg** beginning; **alt** alternate; **rep** repeat; **M1** make a stitch by picking up horizontal loop lying before next stitch and working into back of it; **cm** centimetres; **in** inches; **mm** millimetres; **MS** main shade.

NOTE

When working in patt from chart, read odd rows K from right to left and even rows P from left to right. Strand yarns loosely across back of work over not more than 3 sts at a time to keep fabric elastic. Twist yarns on wrong side when changing colours to avoid a hole.

BACK

With No. 3¼mm needles and MS, cast on 98[104,110,116] sts and work in K1, P1 rib for 7cm.
Next row – Rib 9[8,11,10] sts, (M1, rib 4) 20[22,22,24] times, M1, rib to end. *119[127,133,141] sts.*

Change to No. 4mm needles and joining in and breaking off colours as required, work in patt from chart (see p. 76), rep the 24 patt sts 4[5,5,5] times across row and working first 11[3,6,10] sts and last 12[4,7,11] sts on K rows, and first 12[4,7,11] sts and last 11[3,6,10] sts on P rows as indicated.

B I L L Y

MAN'S COLOUR-
PATTERNED
SLIPOVER

*Straight from the
early movies, a
distinctive Fair Isle
design – and a
traditional shape in
a league of its own.*

1 9 2 7

To fit chest				
cm	91	97	102	107
in	36	38	40	42

Garment measures				
cm	91	97	102	107
in	36	38	40	42

Length from top of shoulders				
cm	58	59	60	61
in	23	23	23½	24

Patons Diploma DK

Main shade	50g balls	3	4	4	4
1st contrast	50g balls	2	2	2	2
2nd contrast	50g balls	2	2	2	3
3rd contrast	50g balls	1	1	1	1

Continue in patt until Back measures 35cm, ending with right side facing for next row.

Keeping patt correct, **shape armholes** by casting off 4 sts at beg of next 2 rows, then dec 1 st at each end of next 5[7,9,11] rows. Work 1 row.
Now dec 1 st at each end of next and following 2 alt rows. *95[99,101,105] sts.* **.
Continue in patt until Back measures 58[59,60,61]cm, ending with right side facing for next row.

Shape shoulders by casting off 8[9,10,9] sts at beg of next 2 rows, then 9[9,9,10] sts at beg of following 4 rows.
Leave remaining 43[45,45,47] sts on a spare needle.

FRONT

Work as for Back to **.
Work 3 rows, ending with right side facing for next row.

Keeping patt correct **divide for neck** as follows:
Next row – Patt 39[40,41,42] sts, K2 tog, turn and leave remaining sts on a spare needle.
Continue on these 40[41,42,43] sts for first side and dec 1 st at neck edge on next 8 rows.
Work 1 row.
Now dec 1 st at neck edge on next and following 5 alt rows. *26[27,28,29] sts.*
Work straight until Front matches Back to shoulder, ending with right side facing for next row.

Shape shoulder by casting off 8[9,10,9] sts at beg of next row, then 9[9,9,10] sts at beg of following 2 alt rows.

KEY

◨ = MS

◤ = 1ST CONTRAST

☐ = 2ND CONTRAST

⊡ = 3RD CONTRAST

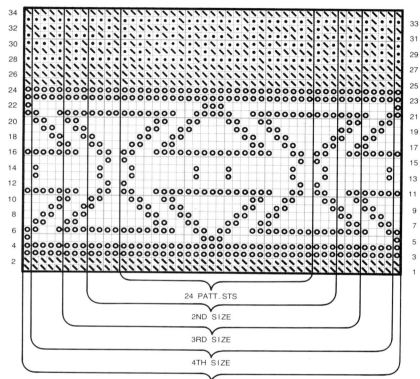

24 PATT.STS

2ND SIZE

3RD SIZE

4TH SIZE

1ST SIZE

With right side facing, slip centre 13[15,15,17] sts on a length of yarn, rejoin appropriate colour yarn to remaining sts, K2 tog, patt to end. Finish to match first side, reversing shapings.

TO MAKE UP

With wrong side of work facing, block each piece by pinning out round edges and, omitting ribbing, press parts lightly following instructions on yarn labels. Join right shoulder seam.

NECKBAND

With right side facing, No. 3¼mm needles and MS, knit up 38[39,39,40] sts down left side of neck, K13[15,15,17] sts from centre, dec 2 sts evenly, knit up 38[39,39,40] sts up right side of neck, then K43[45,45,47] sts from back, dec 4 sts evenly, *126[132,132,138] sts.* Work in K1, P1 rib for 6 rows. Cast off evenly in rib. Join neckband and left shoulder seam.

ARMHOLE BORDERS

With right side facing, No. 3¼mm needles and MS, knit up 104[108,114,118] sts and work in K1, P1 rib for 6 rows. Cast off evenly in rib. Join armhole borders and side seams. Press seams.

MARCELLA

WOMAN'S CAP AND SCARF

Ideal for motoring with the hood down...

---

1 9 3 3

MATERIALS

Cap: 2 50g balls **Patons Beehive DK**.

Scarf: 2 50g balls **Patons Beehive DK**.

Pair No. 4mm needles.

MEASUREMENTS

Cap: width round head 54cm (approx 21½in); depth 19cm (approx 7½in).

TENSION

On No. 4mm needles, 22 sts and 32 rows to 10cm over patt.

ABBREVIATIONS

K knit; **P** purl; **st** stitch; **tog** together; **inc** increase; **beg** beginning; **rep** repeat; **patt** pattern; **cm** centimetres; **in** inches; **mm** millimetres.

CAP

Cast on 60 sts and work in patt as follows:

1st row (right side) – K1, P to last st, K1.
2nd row – K.
Rep 1st and 2nd rows once more.
5th row – K.
6th row – K1, P to last st, K1.
These 6 rows form patt.
Rep these 6 rows until work measures 37cm, ending with a 6th row.
Now rep 1st and 2nd rows once, then 1st row again. Cast off knitways.

SCARF

Cast on 31 sts and work in patt as follows:
1st row (right side) – K1, P2 tog, P to last 2 sts, inc in next st, K1.
2nd row – K.
Rep 1st and 2nd rows once more.
5th row – K1, K2 tog, K to last 2 sts, inc in next st, K1.
6th row – K1, P to last st, K.
These 6 rows form patt.
Rep these 6 rows until work measures 113cm, ending with a 6th row.
Now rep 1st and 2nd rows once, then 1st row again.
Cast off knitways.

TO MAKE UP

Do not press.
Fold work with the cast-on edge to the cast-off edge. Join side seams. Tuck corners of cap inside and join points to side seams at lower edge of cap.

MATERIALS

Pair each No. 3¼mm and No. 4mm needles.

TENSION

On No. 4mm needles, 22 sts and 30 rows to 10cm over stocking stitch.

ABBREVIATIONS

K knit; **P** purl; **sts** stitches; **dec** decrease; **inc** increase; **tog** together; **M1** make a stitch by picking up horizontal loop lying before next stitch and working into back of it; **rep** repeat; **patt** pattern; **alt** alternate; **beg** beginning; **cm** centimetres; **in** inches; **mm** millimetres.

BACK

With No. 3¼mm needles, cast on 96[102,108,114,120] sts and work in K1, P1 rib for 6cm.
Next row – Rib 7[6,9,7,6] (M1, rib 9[10,10,11,12]) 9 times, M1, rib to end. *106[112,118,124,130] sts.*

Change to No. 4mm needles and work in patt as follows:
1st row (right side) – K4[3,2,5,4], *P2, K6; rep from * to last 6[5,4,7,6] sts, P2, K4[3,2,5,4].
2nd row – P.
These 2 rows form patt.
Continue in patt until Back measures 42cm, ending with right side facing for next row.

Keeping patt correct, **shape armholes** by casting off 3 sts at beg of next 2 rows, then dec 1 st at each end of following 5[7,7,7,9] rows. Work 1 row.
Now dec 1 st at each end of next and following 2[2,3,4,4] alt rows. *84[86,90,94,96] sts.* **.

R   O   N

MAN'S ROUND-NECKED SWEATER WITH RIB DETAIL

A classic in every way. This timeless sweater finds a niche in every man's casual English wardrobe.

1   9   3   5

To fit chest					
cm	91	97	102	107	112
in	36	38	40	42	44

Garment measures					
cm	96	102	107	112	118
in	38	40	42	44	46½

Length from top of shoulders					
cm	64	65	66	67	68
in	25	25½	26	26½	27

Sleeve seam					
cm	46	46	47	47	47
in	18	18	18½	18½	18½

Patons Beehive DK

50g balls		10	11	11	12	12

Work straight until Back measures 64[65,66,67,68]cm, ending with right side facing for next row.

Shape shoulders by casting off 8[8,7,9,9] sts at beg of next 2 rows, then 7[7,8,8,8] sts at beg of following 4 rows.
Leave remaining 40[42,44,44,46] sts on a spare needle.

FRONT

Work as for Back to **.
Work straight until Front measures 55[56,57,58,59]cm, ending with right side facing for next row.

Divide for neck as follows:
Next row – Patt 31[31,32,34,34], work 2 tog, turn and leave remaining sts on a spare needle.
Continue on these 32[32,33,35,35] sts for first side and dec 1 st at neck edge on next 6 rows. Work 1 row. Now dec 1 st at neck edge on next and following 3 alt rows. *22[22,23,25,25] sts.*
Work straight until Front matches Back to shoulder, ending with right side facing for next row.

Shape shoulder by casting off 8[8,7,9,9] sts at beg of next row, then 7[7,8,8,8] sts at beg of following 2 alt rows.
With right side facing, leave centre 18[20,22,22,24] sts on a length of yarn, rejoin yarn to remaining sts, work 2 tog, patt to end.
Finish to correspond with first side.

SLEEVES

With No. 3¼mm needles, cast on 48[50,50,52,54] sts and work in K1, P1 rib for 6cm.
Next row – Rib 4[5,5,6,4], (M1, rib

8[8,8,8,9]) 5 times, M1, rib to end.
54[56,56,58,60] sts.

Change to No. 4mm needles and
place the patt as for
3rd[2nd,2nd,1st,4th] size on Back,
shaping sides by inc 1 st at each end
of 9th[9th,3rd,3rd,3rd] and every
following 9th row until there are
78[80,82,84,86] sts, taking increased
sts into patt.

Work straight until sleeve seam
measures 46[46,47,47,47]cm, ending
with right side facing for next row.

Keeping patt correct, **shape top** by
casting off 3 sts at beg of next 2

rows, then dec 1 st at each end of
following row. Work 1[1,3,3,3] rows.

5th size only

Rep last 4 rows once more.

All sizes

Now dec 1 st at each end of next and
every alt row until 22 sts remain.
Cast off.

TO MAKE UP

Do not press.
Join right shoulder seam.

NECKBAND

With right side facing and No. 3¼
mm needles, knit up 24 sts down left
side of neck, K18[20,22,22,24] sts
from centre front, knit up 24 sts up
right side, then K40[42,44,44,46] sts
from back. *106[110,114,114,118] sts.*
Work in K1, P1 rib for 2 or 5cm,
according to preference. Cast off
evenly in rib.

Join left shoulder seam and
neckband, side and sleeve seams.
Insert sleeves.
If neckband is 5cm in depth, fold
neckband in half to wrong side and
slip hem loosely in position all
round.

MATERIALS
Pair No. 2¾mm needles.

TENSION
On No. 2¾mm needles, 32 sts and 40 rows to 10cm.

ABBREVIATIONS
K knit; **P** purl; **sts** stitches; **tog** together; **inc** increase; **dec** decrease; **beg** beginning; **alt** alternate; **rep** repeat; **patt** pattern; **cm** centimetres; **in** inches; **mm** millimetres; **A** main shade; **B** 1st contrast; **C** 2nd contrast.

NOTE
When working colour patt, use separate balls of yarn, twisting yarn when changing colour to avoid a hole.

SOCKS
With A, cast on 81 sts.
1st row (right side) – K1, *P1, K1; rep from * to end.
2nd row – P1, *K1, P1; rep from * to end.
Rep these 2 rows until work measures 18cm, ending with a 2nd row and inc 1 st at centre. *82 sts.* Joining in and breaking off colours as required, work in patt as follows:

1st row – K2 tog in A, K25 in B, 1 A, 12 B, K2 tog B, 12 B, 1 A, 25 B, K2 tog A. *79 sts.*
2nd row – P2 A, (23 B, 3 A) twice, 23 B, 2 A.
3rd row – K1 A, (2 A, 21 B, 3 A) 3 times.
4th row – P4 A, (19 B, 7 A) twice, 19 B, 4 A.
5th row – K1 A, (4 A, 17 B, 5 A) 3 times.

ROGER

MAN'S GOLF SOCKS

The sort of socks that most men only dream of – now you have the pattern, he need dream no longer. They are knitted in stocking stitch on two needles.

1 9 3 5

Foot length			
cm	25	27	28
in	10	10½	11

Length from top to heel			
cm	49	49	49
in	19½	19½	19½

Patons Clansman 4 ply

Main shade (A)	50g balls	2	2	2
1st contrast (B)	50g balls	1	1	1
2nd contrast (C)	50g balls	1	1	1

6th row – P6 A, (15 B, 11 A) twice, 15 B, 6 A.
7th row – K1 A, (6 A, 13 B, 7 A) 3 times.
8th row – P8 A, (11 B, 15 A) twice, 11 B, 8 A.
9th row – K1 A, (8 A, 9 B, 9 A) 3 times.
10th row – P10 A, (7 B, 19 A) twice, 7 B, 10 A.

11th row – K1 A, (10 A, 5 B, 11 A) 3 times.
12th row – P12 A, (3 B, 23 A) twice, 3 B, 12 A.
13th row – K1 A, (12 A, 1 B, 13 A) 3 times.
14th row – P to end in A.
15th row – K1 A, (12 A, 1 C, 13 A) 3 times.

16th row – P12 A, (3 C, 23 A) twice, 3 C, 12 A.
17th row – K1 A, (10 A, 5 C, 11 A) 3 times.
18th row – P10 A, (7 C, 19 A) twice, 7 C, 10 A.
19th row – K1 A, (8 A, 9 C, 9 A) 3 times.
20th row – P8 A, (11 C, 15 A) twice, 11 C, 8 A.

21st row – K1 A, (6 A, 13 C, 7 A) 3 times.
22nd row – P6 A, (15 C, 11 A) twice, 15 C, 6 A.
23rd row – K1 A, (4 A, 17 C, 5 A) 3 times.
24th row – P4 A, (19 C, 7 A) twice, 19 C, 4 A.
25th row – K1 A, (2 A, 21 C, 3 A) 3 times.

26th row – P2 A, (23 C, 3 A) twice, 23 C, 2 A.
27th row – K1 A, (25 C, 1 A) 3 times.
28th row – P to end in C.

29th row – K1 B, (25 C, 1 B) 3 times.

30th row – P2 B, (23 C, 3 B) twice, 23 C, 2 B.

31st row – K1 B, (2 B, 21 C, 3 B) 3 times.

32nd row – P4 B, (19 C, 7 B) twice, 19 C, 4 B.

33rd row – K1 B, (4 B, 17 C, 5 B) 3 times.

34th row – P6 B, (15 C, 11 B) twice, 15 C, 6 B.

35th row – K1 B, (6 B, 13 C, 7 B) 3 times.

36th row – P8 B, (11 C, 15 B) twice, 11 C, 8 B.

37th row – K1 B, (8 B, 9 C, 9 B) 3 times.

38th row – P10 B, (7 C, 19 B) twice, 7 C, 10 B.

39th row – K1 B, (10 B, 5 C, 11 B) 3 times.

40th row – P12 B, (3 C, 23 B) twice, 3 C, 12 B.

41st row – K1 B, (12 B, 1 C, 13 B) 3 times.

42nd row – P to end in B.

43rd row – K1 B, (12 B, 1 A, 13 B) 3 times.

44th row – P12 B, (3 A, 23 B) twice, 3 A, 12 B.

45th row – K1 B, (10 B, 5 A, 11 B) 3 times.

46th row – P10 B, (7 A, 19 B) twice, 7 A, 10 B.

47th row – K1 B, (8 B, 9 A, 9 B) 3 times.

48th row – P8 B, (11 A, 15 B) twice, 11 A, 8 B.

49th row – K1 B, (6 B, 13 A, 7 B) 3 times.

50th row – P6 B, (15 A, 11 B) twice, 15 A, 6 B.

51st row – K1 B, K2 tog B, 2 B, (17 A, 9 B) twice, 17 A, 2 B, K2 tog B, 1 B. *77 sts.*

52nd row – P3 B, (19 A, 7 B) twice, 19 A, 3 B.

53rd row – K2 B, (21 A, 5 B) twice, 21 A, 2 B.

54th row – P1 B, (23 A, 3 B) twice, 23 A, 1 B.

55th row – K25 A, (1 B, 25 A) twice.

56th row – P to end in A.

57th row – K1 A, K2 tog A, 10 A, (12 A, 1 C, 13 A) twice, 9 A, K2 tog A, 1 A. *75 sts.*

58th row – P12 A, (11 A, 3 C, 12 A) twice, 11 A.

59th row – K1 C, 11 A, (10 A, 5 C, 11 A) twice, 10 A, 1 C.

60th row – P2 C, 10 A, (9 A, 7 C, 10 A) twice, 9 A, 2 C.

61st row – K3 C, 9 A, (8 A, 9 C, 9 A) twice, 8 A, 3 C.

62nd row – P4 C, 8 A, (7 A, 11 C, 8 A) twice, 7 A, 4 C.

63rd row – K1 C, K2 tog C, 2 C, 7 A, (6 A, 13 C, 7 A) twice, 6 A, 2 C, K2 tog C, 1 C. *73 sts.*

64th row – P5 C, 6 A, (5 A, 15 C, 6 A) twice, 5 A, 5 C.

65th row – K6 C, 5 A, (4 A, 17 C, 5 A) twice, 4 A, 6 C.

66th row – P7 C, 4 A, (3 A, 19 C, 4 A) twice, 3 A, 7 C.

67th row – K8 C, 3 A, (2 A, 21 C, 3 A) twice, 2 A, 8 C.

68th row – P9 C, 2 A, (1 A, 23 C, 2 A) twice, 1 A, 9 C.
69th row – K1 C, K2 tog C, 7 C, 1 A, (25 C, 1 A) twice, 7 C, K2 tog C, 1 C. *71 sts.*

70th row – P to end in C.
71st row – K9 C, 1 B, (25 C, 1 B) twice, 9 C.
72nd row – P8 C, 2 B, (1 B, 23 C, 2 B) twice, 1 B, 8 C.
73rd row – K7 C, 3 B, (2 B, 21 C, 3 B) twice, 2 B, 7 C.
74th row – P6 C, 4 B, (3 B, 19 C, 4 B) twice, 3 B, 6 C.
75th row – K1 C, K2 tog C, 2 C, 5 B, (4 B, 17 C, 5 B) twice, 4 B, 2 C, K2 tog C, 1 C. *69 sts.*

76th row – P3 C, 6 B, (5 B, 15 C, 6 B) twice, 5 B, 3 C.
77th row – K2 C, 7 B, (6 B, 13 C, 7 B) twice, 6 B, 2 C.
78th row – P1 C, 8 B, (7 B, 11 C, 8 B) twice, 7 B, 1 C.
79th row – K9 B, (8 B, 9 C, 9 B) twice, 8 B.
80th row – P9 B, (9 B, 7 C, 10 B) twice, 8 B.

81st row – K1 B, K2 tog B, 6 B, (10 B, 5 C, 11 B) twice, 5 B, K2 tog B, 1 B. *67 sts.*
82nd row – P8 B, (11 B, 3 C, 12 B) twice, 7 B.
83rd row – K8 B, (12 B, 1 C, 13 B) twice, 7 B.
84th row – P to end in B.
85th row – K8 B, (12 B, 1 A, 13 B) twice, 7 B.
86th row – P8 B, (11 B, 3 A, 12 B) twice, 7 B.
87th row – K1 B, K2 tog B, 5 B, (10 B, 5 A, 11 B) twice, 4 B, K2 tog B, 1 B. *65 sts.*
88th row – P7 B, (9 B, 7 A, 10 B) twice, 6 B.

89th row – K7 B, (8 B, 9 A, 9 B) twice, 6 B.
90th row – P7 B, (7 B, 11 A, 8 B) twice, 6 B.
91st row – K7 B, (6 B, 13 A, 7 B) twice, 6 B.
92nd row – P1 A, 6 B, (5 B, 15 A, 6 B) twice, 5 B, 1 A.
93rd row – K2 A, 5 B, (4 B, 17 A, 5 B) twice, 4 B, 2 A.
94th row – P3 A, 4 B, (3 B, 19 A, 4 B) twice, 3 B, 3 A.
95th row – K4 A, 3 B, (2 B, 21 A, 3 B) twice, 2 B, 4 A.
96th row – P5 A, 2 B, (1 B, 23 A, 2 B) twice, 1 B, 5 A.
97th row – K6 A, 1 B, (25 A, 1 B) twice, 6 A.
98th row – P to end in A.
99th row – K6 A, 1 C, (25 A, 1 C) twice, 6 A.
100th row – P5 A, 2 C, (1 C, 23 A, 2 C) twice, 1 C, 5 A.
101st row – K4 A, 3 C, (2 C, 21 A, 3 C) twice, 2 C, 4 A.
102nd row – P3 A, 4 C, (3 C, 19 A, 4 C) twice, 3 C, 3 A.
103rd row – K2 A, 5 C, (4 C, 17 A, 5 C) twice, 2 C, 4 A.
104th row – P1 A, 6 C, (5 C, 15 A, 6 C) twice, 5 C, 1 A.

105th row – K7 C, (6 C, 13 A, 7 C) twice, 6 C.
106th row – P7 C, (7 C, 11 A, 8 C) twice, 6 C.
107th row – K7 C, (8 C, 9 A, 9 C) twice, 6 C.
108th row – P7 C, (9 C, 7 A, 10 C) twice, 6 C.
109th row – K7 C, (10 C, 5 A, 11 C) twice, 6 C.
110th row – P7 C, (11 C, 3 A, 12 C) twice, 6 C.

111th row – K7 C, (12 C, 1 A, 13 C) twice, 6 C.
112th row – P to end in C.
113th row – K7 C, (12 C, 1 B, 13 C) twice, 6 C.
114th row – P7 C, (11 C, 3 B, 12 C) twice, 6 C.
115th row – K7 C, (10 C, 5 B, 11 C) twice, 6 C.

116th row – P7 C, (9 C, 7 B, 10 C) twice, 6 C.
117th row – K7 C, (8 C, 9 B, 9 C) twice, 6 C.
118th row – P7 C, (7 C, 11 B, 8 C) twice, 6 C.
119th row – K7 C, (6 C, 13 B, 7 C) twice, 6 C.
120th row – P1 B, 6 C, (5 C, 15 B, 6 C) twice, 5 C, 1 B.
121st row – K2 B, 5 C, (4 C, 17 B, 5

C) twice, 4 C, 2 B.
122nd row – P3 B, 4 C, (3 C, 19 B, 4 C) twice, 3 C, 3 B.
123rd row – K4 B, 3 C, (2 C, 21 B, 3 C) twice, 2 C, 4 B.
124th row – P5 B, 2 C, (1 C, 23 B, 2 C) twice, 1 C, 5 B.
125th row – K6 B, 1 C, (25 B, 1 C) twice, 6 B.
126th row – P to end in B.
127th row – K6 B, 1 A, (25 B, 1 A) twice, 6 B.

Shape heel as follows:
1st row – P5 B, 3 A, 11 B, turn.
2nd row – K10 B, 5 A, 4 B.
3rd row – P3 B, 7 A, 8 B, turn.
4th row – K7 B, 9 A, 2 B.
5th row – P1 B, 11 A, 5 B, turn.
6th row – K4 B, 13 A.
7th row – P14 A, 2 B, turn.
8th row – K1 B, 15 A.
9th row – P15 A, turn.
10th and every alt row – K to end in A.

11th row – P14 A, turn.
13th row – P13 A, turn.
15th row – P12 A, turn.
17th row – P11 A, turn.
19th row – P10 A, turn.
21st row – P9 A, turn.
22nd row – K to end in A.
23rd row – P9 A, then P next st tbl, turn.

24th and every alt row – K in A.
25th row – P10 A, then P next st tbl, turn.

Continue in this way working 1 extra st on every P row until there are 19 sts on needle, turn and work as follows:
1st row – K19 A.
2nd row – P19 A, 12 B, 3 A, 23 B, 3 A, 5 B. *65 sts.*
3rd row – K4 B, 5 A, 10 B, turn.

4th row – P9 B, 7 A, 3 B.
5th row – K2 B, 9 A, 7 B, turn.
6th row – P6 B, 11 A, 1 B.
7th row – K13 A, 4 B, turn.
8th row – P3 B, 14 A.
9th row – K15 A, 1 B, turn.
10th and every alt row – P to end in A.
11th row – K15 A, turn.
13th row – K14 A, turn.
15th row – K13 A, turn.
17th row – K12 A, turn.
19th row – K11 A, turn.
21st row – K10 A, turn.
23rd row – K9 A, turn.
24th row – P to end in A.
25th row – K9 A, then K next st tbl, turn.

26th and every alt row – P in A.

Continue in this way, working 1 extra st on every K row until there are 19 sts on needle, turn and work as follows:
1st row – P19 A.
2nd row – K19 A, 11 B, 5 A, 11 B, 19 A. *65 sts.*
3rd row – P19 A, 10 B, 7 A, 10 B, 19 A.
4th row – K19 A, 9 B, 9 A, 9 B, 19 A.
5th row – P19 A, 8 B, 11 A, 8 B, 19 A.

6th row – K19 A, 7 B, 13 A, 7 B, 19 A.
7th row – P19 A, 6 B, 15 A, 6 B, 19 A.
8th row – K19 A, 5 B, 17 A, 5 B, 19 A.
9th row – P19 A, 4 B, 19 A, 4 B, 19 A.
10th row – K19 A, 3 B, 21 A, 3 B, 19 A.
11th row – P19 A, 2 B, 23 A, 2 B, 19 A.

12th row – K19 A, 1 B, 25 A, 1 B, 19 A.
13th row – P to end in A.
14th row – K19 A, 1 C, 25 A, 1 C, 19 A.
15th row – P19 A, 2 C, 23 A, 2 C, 19 A.

16th row – K19 A, 3 C, 21 A, 3 C, 19 A.
17th row – P19 A, 4 C, 19 A, 4 C, 19 A.
18th row – K19 A, 5 C, 17 A, 5 C, 19 A.
19th row – P19 A, 6 C, 15 A, 6 C, 19 A.
20th row – K19 A, 7 C, 13 A, 7 C, 19 A.

21st row – P19 A, 8 C, 11 A, 8 C, 19 A.
22nd row – K19 A, 9 C, 9 A, 9 C, 19 A.
23rd row – P19 A, 10 C, 7 A, 10 C, 19 A.
24th row – K19 A, 11 C, 5 A, 11 C, 19 A.
25th row – P19 A, 12 C, 3 A, 12 C, 19 A.

26th row – K19 A, 13 C, 1 A, 13 C, 19 A.
27th row – P19 A, 27 C, 19 A.
28th row – K19 A, 13 C, 1 B, 13 C, 19 A.
29th row – P19 A, 12 C, 3 B, 12 C, 19 A.
30th row – K19 A, 11 C, 5 B, 11 C, 19 A.

31st row – P19 A, 10 C, 7 B, 10 C, 19 A.
32nd row – K19 A, 9 C, 9 B, 9 C, 19 A.
33rd row – P19 A, 8 C, 11 B, 8 C, 19 A.
34th row – K19 A, 7 C, 13 B, 7 C, 19 A.

35th row – P19 A, 6 C, 15 B, 6 C, 19 A.
36th row – K19 A, 5 C, 17 B, 5 C, 19 A.
37th row – P19 A, 4 C, 19 B, 4 C, 19 A.
38th row – K19 A, 3 C, 21 B, 3 C, 19 A.
39th row – P19 A, 2 C, 23 B, 2 C, 19 A.
40th row – K19 A, 1 C, 25 B, 1 C, 19 A.

41st row – P19 A, 27 B, 19 A.
42nd row – K20 A, 25 B, 20 A.
43rd row – P21 A, 23 B, 21 A.
44th row – K22 A, 21 B, 22 A.
45th row – P23 A, 19 B, 23 A.

46th row – K24 A, 17 B, 24 A.
47th row – P25 A, 15 B, 25 A.
48th row – K26 A, 13 B, 26 A.

49th row – P27 A, 11 B, 27 A.
50th row – K28 A, 9 B, 28 A.

51st row – P29 A, 7 B, 29 A.
52nd row – K30 A, 5 B, 30 A.
53rd row – P31 A, 3 B, 31 A.
54th row – K32 A, 1 B, 32 A. Break off B.
55th row – P32, P2 tog, P31. *64 sts.*
Continue in A only and stocking stitch until foot measures 15[16,18]cm from last turning row of instep, ending with a P row.

Shape toe as follows:
1st row – (K13, K2 tog, K2, K2 tog tbl, K13) twice.
2nd and every alt row – P.
3rd row – (K12, K2 tog, K2, K2 tog tbl, K12) twice.
5th row – (K11, K2 tog, K2, K2 tog tbl, K11) twice.

7th row – (K10, K2 tog, K2, K2 tog tbl, K10) twice.
9th row – (K9, K2 tog, K2, K2 tog tbl, K9) twice.
11th row – (K8, K2 tog, K2, K2 tog tbl, K8) twice.

13th row – (K7, K2 tog, K2, K2 tog tbl, K7) twice.
15th row – (K6, K2 tog, K2, K2 tog tbl, K6) twice.
16th row – P.
Cast off.

Work another in same way.

TO MAKE UP

Press on wrong side following instructions on yarn label. Join back seams and across toe.

RUG

MATERIALS

8 50g balls **Patons Beehive Chunky** in first colour and 2 50g balls in second colour.
2 50g **Patons Beehive Chunky Twirl** for each of the third and fourth colours.
Pair of No. 6mm needles.

MEASUREMENTS

Length 138cm (54½in); width approx 86cm (34in).

TENSION

On No. 6mm needles, 20 sts and 21 rows to 10cm over K1, P1 rib.

ABBREVIATIONS

K knit; **P** purl; **sts** stitches; **rep** repeat; **cm** centimetres; **in** inches; **mm** millimetres; **A** 1st colour; **B** 2nd colour; **C** 3rd colour; **D** 4th colour.

RUG

With No. 6mm needles and B, cast on 173 sts and work as follows:
1st row (right side) – K2, *P1, K1; rep from * to last st, K1.
2nd row – K1, *P1, K1; rep from * to end.
Rep last 2 rows 7 times more. Break off B, join in C.
Rep 1st and 2nd rows 8 times. Break off C, join in A.
Rep 1st and 2nd rows 8 times. Break off A, join in D.
Rep 1st and 2nd rows 8 times. Break off D, join in A.
Rep 1st and 2nd rows until Rug measures 108cm, ending with a 2nd row. Break off A, join in D.

MAYFAIR

MATCHING MULTI-COLOURED RUG, GAUNTLET GLOVES AND SOCKS

Take the chill off rugby matches, picnics, open-air concerts...

1 9 3 3

Rep 1st and 2nd rows 8 times. Break off D, join in A.
Rep 1st and 2nd rows 8 times. Break off A, join in C.
Rep 1st and 2nd rows 8 times. Break off C, join in B.
Rep 1st and 2nd rows 7 times, then 1st row again.
Cast off evenly in B.

GLOVES

MATERIALS

2 50g balls of **Patons Clansman DK**.
Set of No. 4mm needles with points at both ends.

MEASUREMENTS

Measurement around hand below fingers, 18cm (7in).

TENSION

On No. 4mm needles, 22 sts and 30 rounds to 10cm over stocking stitch.

ABBREVIATIONS

K knit; **P** purl; **sts** stitches; **tog** together; **cm** centimetres; **in** inches; **mm** millimetres; **rep** repeat; **inc** increase.

RIGHT GLOVE

Cast on 66 sts and divide equally between 3 needles (22 sts on each).
1st round – *K1, P1; rep from * to end.
Rep last round until work measures 15cm.
Next round – K1, (P2 tog, K2 tog) 16 times, P1. *34 sts.*
Next round – *K1, P1; rep from * to end.
Rep last round 5 times more.
Next round – (K4, inc in next st) 6 times, K4. *40 sts.*
K 16 rounds. **.

Make thumb opening as follows:
Next round – K1, slip next 5 sts on to a safety-pin, cast on 5 sts, K to end of round.
*** K 14 rounds.

Work first finger as follows:
Next round – K6, leave next 28 sts on a spare needle, cast on 1 st, K last 6 sts.
K 19 rounds on these 13 sts.
Next round – K2 tog, 6 times, K1.
Break off yarn, thread through remaining sts, draw up tightly and fasten off securely.

Work second finger as follows:
Next round – K next 5 sts of round, cast on 1 st, K last 5 sts of round, then knit up 1 st at base of first finger.
K 23 rounds on these 12 sts.
Next round – K2 tog, 6 times.
Finish as for first finger.

Work third finger as follows:

Next round – K next 5 sts of round, cast on 1 st, K last 5 sts of round, then knit up 1 st at base of second finger.

K 21 rounds on these 12 sts.

Next round – K2 tog, 6 times. Finish as for first finger.

Work fourth finger as follows:
Next round – K the remaining 8 sts and knit up 1 st from base of third finger.

K 15 rounds on these 9 sts.

Next round – K2 tog 4 times, K1. Finish as for first finger.

Work thumb as follows:
K the 5 sts from safety-pin, then knit up 9 sts round the opening.

K 17 rounds on these 14 sts.

Next round – K2 tog 7 times. Finish as for first finger.

LEFT GLOVE

Work as for Right Glove to **.

Make thumb opening as follows:
Next round – K to last 6 sts, slip next 5 sts on to a safety-pin, cast on 5 sts, K1.

Finish as Right Glove from *** to end.

Brush 15cm rib with teasel brush until a fluffy appearance is achieved.

SOCKS

MATERIALS

2[2,2,3] 50g balls of **Patons Clansman DK**.

Set of 4 No. 4mm needles with points at both ends.

MEASUREMENTS

Foot length 22[23,24,25]cm (approx 8½[9,9½,10]in).

TENSION

On No. 4mm needles, 22 sts and 30 rows to 10cm over stocking stitch.

ABBREVIATIONS

K knit; **P** purl; **sts** stitches; **tog** together; **tbl** through back of loops; **sl** slip; **psso** pass slipped stitch over; **rep** repeat; **cm** centimetres; **in** inches; **mm** millimetres.

SOCKS

Cast on 14 sts on each of first and 2nd needles, then 16 on the 3rd. *44 sts.*

1st round – *K1, P1; rep from * to end.

Rep last round until work measures 17cm.

K 4 rounds.

Next round – K11, then slip the last 11 sts of round on to the same needle that first 11 sts were knitted on to (these 22 sts are for heel).

Divide remaining 22 sts on to two needles and leave for instep.

Work on heel sts as follows:
1st row – P.
2nd row – K.

Rep last 2 rows 9 times more, then 1st row again.

Turn heel as follows:
1st row – K13, sl 1, K1, psso, turn.
2nd row – P5, P2 tog, turn.
3rd row – K5, sl 1, K1, psso, turn.

Rep 2nd and 3rd rows until all sts are knitted in, ending with the 2nd row.

Place all 22 instep sts on to one needle.

Next round – K3 heel sts; using a spare needle, K last 3 heel sts, then on to same needle knit up 11 sts up side of heel; with a 2nd needle, K all

22 instep sts; with a 3rd needle, knit up 11 sts down side of heel, then K first 3 heel sts. *50 sts.*
Work as follows:
1st round – K.
2nd round – K to last 3 sts on first needle, K2 tog, K1, K 22 sts on 2nd needle, K1, K2 tog tbl, K to end of 3rd needle.
3rd round – K.
Rep last 3 rounds twice. *44 sts.*
K every round for 11[12,13,14]cm.

Work toe as follows:
1st round – K to last 3 sts on first needle, K2 tog tbl, K2, K2 tog, K to last 3 sts on 2nd needle, K2 tog tbl, K2, K2 tog, K to end.
2nd round – K.
Rep last 2 rounds 4 times more, then 1st round again. *20 sts.*
Cast off. Make another in the same way.

TO MAKE UP

Join toe seam by folding toe (right sides together) with decreasings at sides, then join cast-off edges neatly. Fold ribbing in half to right side and brush ribbing facing to the outside with a teasel brush until a fluffy appearance is achieved.

R O M A

WOMAN'S
THREE-QUARTER
LENGTH COAT

*A stunning country
classic, straight
from the twenties.*

1 9 2 0

To fit bust

cm	81	86	91	97	102
in	32	34	36	38	40

Garment measures

cm	93	98	103	109	114
in	36½	38½	40½	43	45

Length from shoulder

cm	79	80	80	81	81
in	31	31½	31½	32	32

Sleeve seam, with cuff turned back

cm	43	43	44	44	46
in	17	17	17½	17½	18

Patons Clansman DK

50g balls		15	15	16	16	17

MATERIALS

Pair each No. 3¼mm and No. 4mm
needles.
2 buttons.

TENSION

On No. 4mm needles, 22 sts and 30
rows to 10cm over stocking stitch.

ABBREVIATIONS

K knit; **P** purl; **st** stitch; **tog** together;
tbl through back of loops;
inc increase; **dec** decrease;
beg beginning, **alt** alternate;
rep repeat; **patt** pattern; **sl 1** slip one
stitch; **cm** centimetres; **in** inches;
mm millimetres.

BACK

With No. 3¼mm needles, cast on
112[118,124,130,136] sts and,
starting with a K row, work 13 rows
in stocking stitch.
Next row – K. (This row forms
hemline.)

Change to No. 4mm needles and,
starting with a K row, work 46 rows
in stocking stitch.

Shape sides as follows:
Next row – K6, K2 tog tbl, K to last
8 sts, K2 tog, K6.
Work 23 rows.
Rep last 24 rows until
102[108,114,120,126] sts remain.
Work straight until Back measures
58[58,57,57,56]cm from hemline,
ending with a P row.

Shape armholes by casting off
6[7,7,8,8] sts at beg of next 2 rows.
Dec 1 st at each end of next and
every alt row until 74[76,80,82,86]
sts remain.

Work straight until Back measures

79[80,80,81,81]cm from hemline,
ending with a P row.

Shape shoulders by casting off
7[7,7,7,8] sts at beg of next 4 rows,
then 7[7,8,8,7] sts at beg of following
2 rows.
Cast off remaining 32[34,36,38,40]
sts.

LEFT FRONT

With No. 3¼mm needles, cast on
63[66,69,72,75] sts and, starting with
a K row, work 13 rows in stocking
stitch. **.
Next row – Cast on 22 sts for
facing, P across these 22 sts, K to
end. (This row forms hemline.)
85[88,91,94,97] sts.

Change to No. 4mm needles and
work as follows:
1st row – K to last 23 sts, sl 1, K22.
2nd row – P.
Rep last 2 rows 22 times more.

Shape side as follows:
Next row – K6, K2 tog tbl, K to last
23 sts, sl 1, K22.
Work 23 rows keeping continuity of
sl st on every alt row.
Rep last 24 rows until
80[83,86,89,92] sts remain.
Work straight until Front measures
same as Back to start of armhole
shaping, ending with a P row.

Shape armhole by casting off
6[7,7,8,8] sts at beg of next row.
Work 1 row.
Dec 1 st at armhole edge on next and
every alt row until 66[67,69,70,72]
sts remain.
Work straight until Front measures
73[74,74,75,75]cm from hemline,
ending with a P row.

Shape neck as follows:
Next row – K34[35,37,37,38], turn

and leave remaining sts on a spare needle.
Dec 1 st at neck edge on every row until 21[21,22,22,23] sts remain. Work straight until Front measures same as Back to start of shoulder shaping, ending with a P row.

Shape shoulder by casting off 7[7,7,7,8] sts at beg of next and following alt row.
Work 1 row.
Cast off remaining 7[7,8,8,7] sts.
With right side facing, rejoin yarn to remaining sts from spare needle, cast off 19[19,19,21,23] sts, K to end.
Dec 1 st at *end* of next and every row at same edge until 2 sts remain.
Work 2 tog and fasten off.

RIGHT FRONT

Work as for Left Front to **.
Next row – K to end, cast on 22 sts for facing. (This row forms hemline.) *85[88,91,94,97] sts.*

Change to No. 4mm needles and work as follows:
1st row – K22, sl 1, K to end.
2nd row – P.
Rep last 2 rows 22 times more.

Shape side as follows:
Next row – K22, sl 1, K to last 8 sts, K2 tog, K6.
Work 23 rows keeping continuity of sl st on every alt row.
Rep last 24 rows until 80[83,86,89,92] sts remain.
Work straight until Front measures same as Back to start of armhole shaping, ending with a K row.

Shape armhole by casting off 6[7,7,8,8] sts at beg of next row.
Dec 1 st at armhole edge on next and every alt row until 66[67,69,70,72] sts remain.
Work straight until Front measures 73[74,74,75,75]cm from hemline, ending with a P row.

Shape neck as follows:
Next row – K13[13,13,12,11], turn and leave remaining sts on a spare needle.

Dec 1 st at *beginning* of next and every row at same edge until 2 sts remain. Work 2 tog and fasten off.

With right side facing, rejoin yarn to sts from spare needle, cast off 19[19,19,21,23] sts, K to end.

Dec 1 st at neck edge on every row until 21[21,22,22,23] sts remain. Work straight until Front measures same as Back to start of shoulder shaping, ending with a K row.

Shape shoulder by casting off 7[7,7,7,8] sts at beg of next and following alt row. Work 1 row. Cast off remaining 7[7,8,8,7] sts.

SLEEVES

With No. 4mm needles, cast on 75[77,81,85,87] sts and K 5 rows. Starting with a P row work 20 rows in reverse stocking stitch for cuff. Place a marker at each end of last row.
Now, starting with a K row, work in stocking stitch until sleeve measures 43[43,44,44,46]cm from markers, ending with a P row.

Shape top as follows:
Cast off 6[7,7,8,8] sts at beg of next 2 rows.
Dec 1 st at each end of next and every following 4th row until 53[51,55,57,57] sts remain. Work 1 row.
Dec 1 st at each end of next and

every alt row until 27 sts remain.
Cast off.

COLLAR

With No. 4mm needles, cast on
92[96,100,104,108] sts and, starting
with a K row, work 22cm in stocking
stitch, ending with a P row.
Cast off.

TO MAKE UP

Press on wrong side following
instructions on yarn label.
Join shoulder and side seams.
Fold hem at lower edge on hemline
to wrong side and slip stitch loosely
in position. Fold facing on sl st line
to wrong side and slip stitch loosely
in position. Neaten lower front
corners.
Sew one edge of collar round neck
edge, fold over and sew other edge in
same way, forming a double collar;
sew together neatly at each end.
Join sleeve seams and set in sleeves.
Sew two buttons to left front approx
12cm and 24cm from lower edge.
Make two button loops to
correspond. Fold collar to right side.
Press seams, collar and facings.

MATERIALS

Pair No. 4mm needles.
6 buttons.

TENSION

On No. 4mm needles, 22 sts and 30 rows to 10cm over stocking stitch.

ABBREVIATIONS

K knit; **P** purl; **st** stitch; **tog** together; **tbl** through back of loops; **inc** increase; **dec** decrease; **beg** beginning; **alt** alternate; **rep** repeat; **patt** pattern; **cm** centimetres; **in** inches; **mm** millimetres.

POCKET LININGS

(make 2)
With No. 4mm needles, cast on 25 sts and beg and ending with a K row, work 10cm in stocking stitch. Break off yarn. Leave sts on a spare needle.

RIGHT FRONT

** With No. 4mm needles, cast on 85[89,91,95,97] sts.
1st row (right side) – K1, *P1, K1; rep from * to end.
2nd row – P1, *K1, P1; rep from * to end, inc 1 st at centre for 1st, 3rd and 5th sizes only.

Now work in stocking stitch, beg with a K row, until work measures 9cm, ending with a P row. **.
Next row (buttonhole) – K18, cast off 2, K8 (including st on needle after cast off), cast off 2, K to end.
Next row – P to end, casting on 2 sts over those cast off. Work 12 rows.
Next row – K54[56,58,62,64], (P1, K1) 12 times, P1, K to end.

A L Y S

**WOMAN'S
SLEEVELESS
JACKET WITH
REVER COLLAR**

*This versatile
waistcoat will top
trousers, shirts,
sweaters, or
dresses – or play
a major part
in a layered outfit.*

1 9 3 5

To fit bust					
cm	81	86	91	97	102
in	32	34	36	38	40

Garment measures					
cm	93	98	103	109	114
in	36½	38½	40½	43	45

Length from shoulder					
cm	65	66	67	68	70
in	25½	26	26½	27	27½

Patons Moorland Tweed DK

50g balls					
		9	9	10	10	11

Next row – P7[8,9,8,9], (K1, P1) 12 times, K1, P to end.
Next row – K54[56,58,62,64], cast off 25 sts in rib, K to end.
Next row – P7[8,9,8,9], P across 25 sts of first Pocket Lining, P to end. Work 2 rows, then make second set of buttonholes as before.
Work 18 rows, then make third set of buttonholes as before.

Shape front edge by inc 1 st at *beginning* of next and every following 16th row until there are 90[93,96,99,102] sts. Work 9 rows ending with a P row.
Now work as follows:
1st row – K to last 4[4,6,6,8] sts, (P1, K1) 2[2,3,3,4] times.
2nd row – K2, (P1, K1) 1[1,2,2,3] times, P to end.
3rd row – K to last 6[6,8,8,10] sts, (P1, K1) 3[3,4,4,5] times.
4th row – K2, (P1, K1) 2[2,3,3,4] times, P to end.
5th row – K to last 8[8,10,10,12] sts, (P1, K1) 4[4,5,5,6] times.

Shape armhole:
Next row – Cast off 4[4,6,6,8], K1, P1, K1, P to end.
Next row – Inc in first st, K to last 6 sts, K2 tog, (P1, K1) twice.
Next row – K2, P1, K1, P to end.
Next row – K to last 6 sts, K2 tog, (P1, K1) twice.
Rep last 2 rows, *at the same time* inc 1 st at front edge on following 16th row from previous inc until 79[81,82,84,85] sts remain.

1st size only

Work 1 row, then inc 1 st at beg of next row. *80 sts.*

All sizes

Work 4[2,2,0,0] rows, ending with wrong side facing for next row.

Divide for front facing as follows:
Next row – K2, P1, K1, P46[47,48,50,51], turn and leave remaining 30 sts on a holder.

Shape front edge as follows:
1st row – K1, K2 tog, K14, K2 tog tbl, K to last 4 sts, (P1, K1) twice.
2nd row – K2, P1, K1, P to end.
3rd row – K1, K2 tog, K to last 4 sts, (P1, K1) twice.
4th row – As 2nd.
5th row – As 3rd.
6th row – As 2nd.
Rep the last 6 rows until 24[25,26,28,29] sts remain, then rep 2nd and 3rd rows 2[2,3,4,5] times more. *22[23,23,24,24] sts.*
Work 0[2,4,4,6] rows, ending with *wrong* side facing for next row.

Shape shoulder by casting off 4[5,5,5,5] sts at beg of next and following 2 alt rows.
Work 1 row.
Cast off 5[4,4,5,5] sts at beg of next row.
Work 1 row.
Cast off remaining 5[4,4,4,4] sts.

With wrong side facing rejoin yarn to remaining 30 sts from holder, P to end.
Dec 1 st at end of next and every alt row, *at the same time* inc 1 st at

beginning of every following 16th row from previous inc until 8[7,5,4,3] sts remain. Cast off.

LEFT FRONT

Work as given for Right front from ** to **.
Work 14 rows.
Next row – K7[8,9,8,9], (P1, K1) 12 times, P1, K to end.
Next row – P54[56,58,62,64], (K1, P1) 12 times, K1, P to end.
Next row – K7[8,9,8,9], cast off 25 sts in rib, K to end.
Next row – P54[56,58,62,64], P across 25 sts of second Pocket Lining, P to end.
Work 24 rows.

Shape front edge by inc 1 st at *end* of next and every following 16th row until there are 90[93,96,99,102] sts.
Work 9 rows ending with a P row.
Now work as follows:
1st row – (K1, P1) 2[2,3,3,4] times, K to end.
2nd row – P to last 4[4,6,6,8] sts, (K1, P1) 1[1,2,2,3] times, K2.
3rd row – (K1, P1) 3[3,4,4,5] times, K to end.
4th row – P to last 6[6,8,8,10] sts, (K1, P1) 2[2,3,3,4] times, K2.

Shape armhole:
Next row – Cast off 4[4,6,6,8], P1, K1, P1, K to end.
Next row – P to last 4 sts, K1, P1, K2.

Next row – (K1, P1) twice, K2 tog tbl, K to last st, inc in last st.
Next row – P to last 4 sts, K1, P1, K2.
Next row – (K1, P1) twice, K2 tog tbl, K to end.
Rep last 2 rows, at the same time inc 1 st at front edge on following 16th row from previous inc, until 79[81,82,84,85] sts remain.

1st size only

Work 1 row, then inc 1 st at end of next row. *80 sts.*

All sizes

Work 5[3,3,1,1] rows, ending with right side facing for next row.

Divide for front facing as follows:
Next row – (K1, P1) twice, K27[28,29,31,32], K2 tog, K14, K2 tog tbl, K1, turn and leave remaining 30 sts on a holder.

Shape front edge as follows:
1st row – P to last 4 sts, K1, P1, K2.
2nd row – (K1, P1) twice, K to last 3 sts, K2 tog tbl, K1.
3rd row – As 1st row.
4th row – As 2nd row.
5th row – As 1st row.
6th row – (K1, P1) twice, K to last 19 sts, K2 tog, K14, K2 tog tbl, K1.
Rep last 6 rows until 24[25,26,28,29] sts remain, then rep 1st and 2nd rows 2[2,3,4,5] times more.

22[23,23,24,24] *sts.*
Work 1[3,5,5,7] rows, ending with right side facing for next row.

Shape shoulder by casting off 4[5,5,5,5] sts at beg of next and following 2 alt rows. Work 1 row. Cast off 5[4,4,5,5] sts at beg of next row.
Work 1 row.

Cast off remaining 5[4,4,4,4] sts. With right side facing, rejoin yarn to remaining 30 sts from holder, K2 tog, K to end.
Dec 1 st at beg of every alt row, *at the same time* inc 1 st at *end* of every following 16th row from previous inc, until 8[7,5,4,3] sts remain. Cast off.

BACK

With No. 4mm needles, cast on 101[107,113,119,125] sts and work 2 rows in rib as for Right Front, inc 1 st in centre of 2nd row.
102[108,114,120,126] sts.
Now work in stocking stitch, beg with a K row, until 4 rows less than Fronts to start of armhole shaping have been worked, ending with a P row.
1st row – (K1, P1) 2[2,3,3,4] times, K to last 4[4,6,6,8] sts, (P1, K1) 2[2,3,3,4] times.
2nd row – K2 (P1, K1) 1[1,2,2,3] times, P to last 4[4,6,6,8] sts, (K1, P1) 1[1,2,2,3] times, K2.

3rd row – (K1, P1) 3[3,4,4,5] times, K to last 6[6,8,8,10)] sts, (P1, K1) 3[3,4,4,5] times.
4th row – K2, (P1, K1) 2[2,3,3,4] times, P to last 6[6,8,8,10] sts, (K1, P1) 2[2,3,3,4] times, K2.

Shape armholes:
Next row – Cast off 4[4,6,6,8], P1, K1, P1, K to last 8[8,10,10,12] sts, (P1, K1) 4[4,5,5,6] times.

Next row – Cast off 4[4,6,6,8], K1, P1, K1, P to last 4 sts, K1, P1, K2.
Next row – (K1, P1) twice, K2 tog tbl, K to last 6 sts, K2 tog, (P1, K1) twice.
Next row – K2, P1, K1, P to last 4 sts, K1, P1, K2.
Rep the last 2 rows until 78[80,82,86,88] sts remain.

Next row – K2, P1, K1, P to last 4 sts, K1, P1, K2.
Next row – (K1, P1) twice, K to last 4 sts, (P1, K1) twice.

Rep the last 2 rows until Back measures same as Fronts to start of shoulder shaping, ending with right side facing for next row.

Shape shoulders by casting off 4[5,5,5,5] sts at beg of next 6 rows, 5[4,4,5,5] sts at beg of following 2 rows, then 5[4,4,4,4] sts at beg of following 2 rows.
Cast off remaining 34[34,36,38,40] sts.

COLLAR

With No. 4mm needles, cast on 36 sts and, beg with a K row, work in stocking stitch, inc 1 st at each end of 3rd and every alt row until there are 44 sts.
Cast on 19[20,21,22,23] sts at beg of next 2 rows. *82[84,86,88,90] sts.*
Work 5cm on these sts, place a marker at each end of last row, then work a further 5cm, ending with a K row.
Cast off 19[20,21,22,23] sts at beg of next 2 rows.
Dec 1 st at each end of next and every alt row until 36 sts remain.
Work 2 rows. Cast off.

TO MAKE UP

Press on wrong side of work following instructions on yarn label. Sew pocket linings lightly in position on wrong side. Turn facings to wrong side, placing buttonholes together, slip stitch lightly in position and oversew buttonholes. Turn back revers and press. Join side and shoulder seams.
Fold collar in half at markers, and sew in position across back neck and half-way down front revers. Neatly join remainder of revers.
Sew on 3 buttons to correspond with buttonholes, then sew 3 buttons to right front for double-breasted effect. Press collar and seams.

MATERIALS

Pair No. 3¼mm and No. 4mm
needles.

TENSION

On No. 4mm needles, 22 sts and 30
rows to 10cm over stocking stitch.

ABBREVIATIONS

K knit; **P** purl; **sts** stitches;
tog together; **inc** increase;
dec decrease; **beg** beginning;
alt alternate; **rep** repeat; **patt** pattern;
cm centimetres; **in** inches;
mm millimetres; **M1** make a stitch
by picking up horizontal loop lying
before next stitch and working into
back of it; **A** shade A; **B** shade B;
C shade C; **D** shade D; **E** shade E.

NOTE

When working colour patt use
separate balls of yarn, twisting yarns
on wrong side of work when
changing colour to avoid a hole.

BACK

** With No. 3¼mm needles, cast on
7[10,9,11] sts in A, then on to same
needle cast on 5 sts in C,
16[16,18,18] sts in A, 5 sts in C,
16[16,18,18] sts in A, 5 sts in C,
16[16,18,18] sts in A, 5 sts in C,
16[16,18,18] sts in A, 5 sts in C, and
7[10,9,11] sts in A. *103[109,115,121]
sts.*
Work in rib as follows:
1st row (right side) – K1[0,1,0] in A,
(P1, K1) 3[5,4,6] times in A, P1 in C,
(K1, P1) twice in C, (K1, P1) 8[8,9,9]
times in A, K1 in C, (P1, K1) twice
in C, (P1, K1) 8[8,9,9] times in A, P1
in C, (K1, P1) twice in C, (K1, P1)
8[8,9,9] times in A, K1 in C, (P1,

VERONICA

WOMAN'S
GEOMETRIC
SWEATER

*Just a touch of
Mondrian in the
dramatic contrasts
of this outstanding
sweater.*

1 9 2 6

To fit bust

cm	81	86	91	97
in	32	34	36	38

Garment measures

cm	93	98	103	109
in	36½	38½	40½	43

Length from shoulder

cm	64	65	66	67
in	25	25½	26	26½

Sleeve seam

cm	43	43	44	44
in	17	17	17½	17½

Patons Diploma DK

Shade A	50g balls	2	2	3	3
Shade B	50g balls	1	1	2	2
Shade C	50g balls	4	4	5	5
Shade D	50g balls	3	3	3	4
Shade E	50g balls	5	6	6	6

K1) twice in C, (P1, K1) 8[8,9,9]
times in A, P1 in C, (K1, P1) twice
in A, K1[0,1,0] in A.
2nd row – P1[0,1,0] in A, (K1, P1)
3[5,4,6] times in A, K1 in C, (P1,
K1) twice in C, (P1, K1) 8[8,9,9]
times in A, P1 in C, (K1, P1) twice
in C, (K1, P1) 8[8,9,9] times in A,
K1 in C, (P1, K1) twice in C, (P1,
K1) 8[8,9,9] times in A, P1 in C,
(K1, P1) twice in C, (K1, P1) 8[8,9,9]
times in A, K1 in C, (P1, K1) twice
in C, (P1, K1) 3[5,4,6] times in A,
P1[0,1,0] in A.
Rep last 2 rows once more.

Change to No. 4mm needles and
work as follows:
Next row (right side) – K7[10,9,12]
in A, K5 in C, *K16[16,18,18] in A,
K5 in C; rep from * to last
7[10,9,12] sts, K7[10,9,12] in A.
Next row – P7[10,9,12] in A, P5 in
C, *P16[16,18,18] in A, P5 in C; rep
from * to last 7[10,9,12] sts,
P7[10,9,12] in A.
Rep last 2 rows 20 times more.
Break off A and join in B as
required.

Next row – K7[10,9,12] in B, K5 in
C, *K16[16,18,18] in B, K5 in C; rep
from * to last 7[10,9,12] sts,
K7[10,9,12] in B.
Next row – P7[10,9,12] in B, P5 in
C, *P16[16,18,18] in B, P5 in C; rep
from * to last 7[10,9,12] sts,
P7[10,9,12] in B.
Rep last 2 rows 5 times more.
Break off B.
Next row – K to end in C.
Next row – P to end in C.
Rep last 2 rows twice more.
Join in D as required.
Next row – K7[10,9,12] in D, K5 in
C, *K16[16,18,18] in D, K5 in C; rep

from * to last 7[10,9,12] sts,
K7[10,9,12] in D.
Next row – P7[10,9,12] in D, P5 in
C, *P16[16,18,18] in D, P5 in C, rep
from * to last 7[10,9,12] sts,
P7[10,9,12] in D.
Rep last 2 rows 14 times more.
Break off D and join in E as
required.

Next row – K7[10,9,12] in E, K5 in
C, *K16[16,18,18] in E, K5 in C; rep
from * to last 7[10,9,12] sts,
K7[10,9,12] in E.
Next row – P7[10,9,12] in E, P5 in
C, *P16[16,17,17] in E, P5 in C; rep
from * to last 7[10,9,12] sts,
P7[10,9,12] in E.
Rep last 2 rows 18[18,19,19] times
more.

Keeping continuity of patt, **shape
armholes** by casting off 4[5,5,6] sts
at beg of next 2 rows.
Dec 1 st at each end of next 3 rows.
Work 1 row.

Dec 1 st at each end of next and
following alt row.
Work 1 row.
Break off E and join in D as
required.
Keeping continuity of C stripes and
working in D in place of E, continue
dec 1 st at each end of next and
every alt row until 75[77,81,83] sts
remain.
Work straight in colour sequence as
set until armhole measures
20[21,22,23]cm, from cast off sts,
ending with a P row.

Shape shoulders by casting off
7[7,8,8] sts at beg of next 4 rows,
then 7[8,7,7] sts at beg of following
2 rows. Cast off remaining
33[33,35,37] sts.

FRONT

Work as given for Back from **
until 4 rows less than Back have
been worked to start of armhole
shapings, thus ending with a P row.
Keeping continuity of patt, **divide
for neck** as follows:
Next row – Patt 49[52,55,58] sts, K2
tog, turn and leave remaining sts on
a spare needle.
Work 3 rows on these 50[53,56,59]
sts.

Shape armhole and continue
shaping front neck as follows:
Next row – Cast off 4[5,5,6] sts, patt
to last 2 sts, K2 tog.
Dec 1 st at armhole edge on next 3
rows, then on following 2 alt rows,
at the same time dec 1 st at neck
edge on every following 4th row
from previous dec. *38[40,43,45] sts.*
Work 1 row, thus ending with a P
row.
Break off E and join in D as
required.
Keeping continuity of C stripe and
working D in place of E, continue dec
1 st at armhole edge on next and
every alt row, *at the same time* dec 1
st at neck edge on every following
4th row from previous dec until
31[31,33,33] sts remain.
Keeping armhole edge straight
continue dec 1 st at neck edge as
before until 21[22,23,23] sts remain.
Work straight until Front measures
same as Back to shoulder, ending
with a P row.

Shape shoulder by casting off
7[7,8,8] sts at beg of next and
following alt row. Work 1 row.
Cast off remaining 7[8,7,7] sts.
With right side facing, rejoin C to
remaining sts, K3 tog, patt to end.
Work 3 rows.

Next row – K2 tog, patt to end.
Next row – Cast off 4[5,5,6] sts, patt
to end.
Finish to match first side, reversing
shapings.

SLEEVES

With No. 3¼mm needles and A,
cast on 43[43,45,47] sts and work in
rib as follows:
1st row (right side) – K1, *P1, K1;
rep from * to end.
2nd row – P1, *K1, P1; rep from *
to end.
Rep these 2 rows until rib measures
5cm, ending with a 1st row.
Next row – Rib 4[4,5,6] sts, *M1,
rib 4; rep from * to last 3[3,4,5] sts,
M1, rib to end. *53[53,55,57] sts.*

Change to No. 4mm needles and,
starting with a K row, work in
stocking stitch as follows:
6 rows in B, 6 rows in C, 6 rows in
D and 6 rows in C, at the same time
inc 1 st at each end of 7th and every
following 6th row. *59[59,61,63] sts.*
Break off C, join E and continue in
stocking stitch, inc 1 st at each end
of next and every following
12th[10th,10th,8th] row until there
are 71[75,77,81] sts.
Work straight until sleeve measures
43[43,44,44]cm, ending with a P
row.

Shape top: cast off 4[5,5,6] sts at
beg of next 2 rows.
Dec 1 st at each end of next and
every following 4th row until
57[59,59,61] sts remain.
Work 1 row.
Dec 1 st at each end of next and
every alt row until 23 sts remain.
Cast off.

NECK BORDER

With No. 3¼mm needles and C, cast
on 2 sts.
Work in K1, P1 rib, inc 1 st at
beginning of next and every alt row
until there are 10 sts.
Continue in rib until strip measures
approx 42[44,46,48]cm, ending at
short side.
Dec 1 st at *beginning* of next and
every alt row until 2 sts remain.
Work 2 tog.

TO MAKE UP

Press on wrong side following
instructions on yarn label.
Join shoulder, side and sleeve seams.
Insert sleeves. Join mitred ends of
neck border and sew in position
round neck edge.
Press seams.

TENSION

On No. 4mm needles, 22 sts and 30 rows to 10cm over stocking stitch.

ABBREVIATIONS

K knit; **P** purl; **sts** stitches; **inc** increase; **dec** decrease; **tog** together; **tbl** through back of loops; **M1** make a stitch by picking up horizontal loop lying before next stitch and working into back of it; **patt** pattern; **rep** repeat; **beg** beginning; **alt** alternate; **cm** centimetres; **in** inches; **mm** millimetres; **A** main shade; **B** 1st contrast; **C** 2nd contrast; **D** 3rd contrast.

SWEATER

MATERIALS

Pair each No. 3¼mm and No. 4mm needles.

BACK

With No. 3¼mm needles and A, cast on 84[90,96,102] sts and work in K1, P1 rib for 12cm.
Next row – Rib 3[6,4,7], (M1, rib 7[7,8,8]) 11 times, M1, rib to end. *96[102,108,114] sts.*

Change to No. 4mm needles and, starting with a K row, work in stocking stitch until Back measures 31cm, ending with a P row. Break off A.
Joining in and breaking off colours as required, continue as follows:
1st row – K72[77,81,86] in B, K24[25,27,28] in A.
2nd row – P24[25,27,28] in A, P72[77,81,86] in B.
3rd to 8th rows – Rep 1st and 2nd

R E N E E

WOMAN'S SWEATER, SCARF AND CAP

Guaranteed to bring a sparkle to all sorts of winter activities.

1 9 3 4

To fit bust				
cm	81	86	91	97
in	32	34	36	38
Garment measures				
cm	88	94	99	104
in	34½	37	39	41
Length from top of shoulders				
cm	55	56	57	58
in	21½	22	22½	23
Sleeve seam				
cm	43	43	43	43
in	17	17	17	17

Patons Promise

Main shade (A)				
50g balls		3	3	3	4
1st contrast (B)				
50g balls		1	1	1	1
2nd contrast (C)				
50g balls		4	4	5	5
3rd contrast (D)				
50g balls		1	1	1	1

rows 3 times.
9th row – K72[77,81,86] in D, K24[25,27,28] in A.
10th row – P24[25,27,28] in A, P72[77,81,86] in D.
11th to 16th rows – Rep 9th and 10th rows 3 times.
17th row – In C cast off 3 sts, K to last 24[25,27,28] sts; in A K to end.
18th row – In A cast off 3 sts, P21[22,24,25] (including st on needle after cast off); in C P to end.
19th row – In C K2 tog, K to last 21[22,24,25] sts; in A K to last 2 sts, K2 tog.
20th row – In A P2 tog, P18[19,21,22]; in C P to last 2 sts, P2 tog.
21st row – In C K2 tog, K to last 19[20,22,23] sts; in A K to last 2 sts, K2 tog.
22nd row – In A P2 tog, P16[17,19,20]; in C P to last 2 sts, P2 tog.
23rd row – In C K2 tog, K to last 17[18,20,21] sts; in A K to last 2 sts, K2 tog.
24th row – In A P2 tog, P14[15,17,18]; in C P to last 2 sts, P2 tog.
25th row – In C K2 tog, K13[14,16,17]; in B K to last 2 sts, K2 tog.
26th row – In B P2 tog 0[0,1,1] time, P to last 14[15,17,18] sts; in C P to last 0[0,2,2] sts, P2 tog 0[0,1,1] time.
27th row – In C K2 tog, K12[13,14,15]; in B K to last 2 sts, K2 tog.
28th row – In B P to last 13[14,15,16] sts; in C P to end.
29th row – In C K2 tog, K11[12,13,14]; in B K to last 2 sts, K2 tog.
30th row – In B P to last 12[13,14,15] sts; in C P to end.

31st row – In C K2 tog, K10[11,12,13]; in B K to last 2 sts, K2 tog.
32nd row – In B P to last 11[12,13,14] sts; in C P to end.
33rd row – In C K2 tog 0[1,1,1] time, K11[10,11,12]; in D K to last 0[2,2,2] sts, K2 tog 0[1,1,1] time.
34th row – In D P to last 11[11,12,13] sts; in C P to end.
35th row – In C K2 tog 0[0,1,1] time, K11[11,10,11]; in D K to last 0[0,2,2] sts, K2 tog 0[0,1,1] time.
36th row – In D P to last 11[11,11,12] sts; in C P to end.
37th row – In C K2 tog 0[0,0,1] time, K11[11,11,10]; in D K to last 0[0,0,2] sts, K2 tog 0[0,0,1] time. *70[74,76,80] sts.*
38th row – In D P59[63,65,69]; in C P11.
39th row – In C K11; in D P59[63,65,69].
40th row – As 38th. **

Now continue straight in C only until Back measures 55[56,57,58]cm, ending with a P row.
Shape shoulders by casting off 6[7,7,8] sts at beg of next 2 rows, then 7 sts at beg of following 4 rows. Leave remaining 30[32,34,36] sts on a spare needle.

FRONT

Work as for Back to **.
Now continue straight in C only until Front measures 49[50,51,52]cm, ending with a P row.

Divide for neck as follows:
Next row – K25[26,26,27], K2 tog, turn and leave remaining sts on a spare needle.
Continue on these 26[27,27,28] sts for first side and dec 1 st at neck edge on next 4 rows. Work 1 row.
Now dec 1 st at neck edge on next

and following alt row. *20[21,21,22] sts.*
Work straight until Front matches Back to shoulder, ending with a P row.

Shape shoulder by casting off 6[7,7,8] sts at beg of next row, then 7 sts at beg of following 2 rows.

With right side facing, leave centre 16[18,20,22] sts on a length of yarn, rejoin C yarn to remaining sts, K2 tog, K to end.
Finish to correspond with first side, reversing shapings.

SLEEVES

With No. 3¼mm needles and C, cast on 42[44,44,46] sts and work in K1, P1 rib for 6cm.
Next row – Rib 6[5,5,6] (M1, rib 10[11,11,11]) 3 times, M1, rib to end. *46[48,48,50] sts.*

Change to No. 4mm needles and, starting with a K row, work in stocking stitch, shaping sides by inc 1 st at each end of 11th[11th,9th,9th] and every following 11th[11th,10th,10th] row until there are 64[66,68,70] sts.
Work straight until sleeve seam measures 43cm, ending with a P row.

Shape top by casting off 3 sts at beg of next 2 rows, then dec 1 st at each end of next and 1[2,2,3] following 4th rows. Work 1 row.
Now dec 1 st at each end of next and every alt row until 20 sts remain. Cast off.

TO MAKE UP

Do not press.
Join right shoulder seam.

NECKBAND

With right side facing, No. 3¼mm needles and C, knit up 20 sts down left side of neck, K16[18,20,22] from centre, knit up 20 sts up right side of neck, K30[32,34,36] from back. *86[90,94,98] sts.*
Work in K1, P1 rib for 6cm. Cast off evenly in rib.

Join neckband and left shoulder seam, then join side and sleeve seams. Insert sleeves. Fold neckband in half to wrong side, and slip hem loosely in position all round.

SCARF

MEASUREMENTS

Length excluding fringe 120 cm (47 in); width 15 cm (6 in).

MATERIALS

2 50g balls in 2nd contrast and oddments in main shade and 1st and 3rd contrasts.
Pair No. 4mm needles.
With No. 4mm needles and A, cast on 45 sts and work as follows:
1st row (right side) – K2, *P1, K1; rep from * to last st, K1.
2nd row – K1, *P1, K1; rep from * to end.

Rep last 2 rows 3 times more.
Now work 8 rows rib in C, 8 rows
in D, 8 rows in A, 8 rows in C, and
8 rows in D.
Now continue in B until Scarf
measures 104cm, ending with right
side facing for next row.
Work 8 rows in D, 8 in C, 8 in A, 8
in D, 8 in C, and 8 in A.
Cast off evenly.

Cut C yarn into 18cm lengths and
taking 3 strands together each time
knot along each end to form fringes.

HAT

MATERIALS
Oddments of all four colours.
Pair each No. 3¼mm and No. 4mm
needles.

With No. 3¼mm needles and A,
cast on 75 sts and K 2 rows.
Next row – (K1, M1, K2) 25 times.
100 sts.

Change to No. 4mm needles and
work in K1, P1 rib and stripes of 8
rows A, 8 rows B, 8 rows C, 8 rows
D and 6 rows A.
Next row – In A, K2 tog tbl 50
times.
Next row – In A, *K1, P1; rep from
* to end.
Now work 6 rows rib in B.
Next row – In B, K2 tog tbl 24
times, K1, P1.
Next row – In B, *K1, P1; rep from
* to end.
Now work 6 rows rib in C.
Next row – In C, K2 tog tbl 13
times, break yarn, thread through
remaining sts, draw up tightly and
fasten off securely.

Join seam.

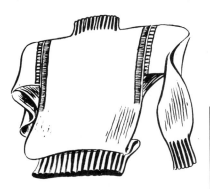

S A M

**TRADITIONAL
GUERNSEY**

*Classic Guernsey
made quick and
easy to knit –
with the
distinctive shoulder
pattern.*

1 9 4 3

To fit bust/chest					
cm	91	97	102	107	112
in	36	38	40	42	44

Garment measures					
cm	104	110	115	120	125
in	41	43½	45½	47	49

Length from top of shoulders					
cm	66	67	68	69	70
in	26	26½	27	27	27½

Sleeve, measured down centre					
cm	48	48	48	48	48
in	19	19	19	19	19

Patons Diploma Aran

50g balls		14	15	15	16	16

MATERIALS

Pair each No. 3¼mm and No. 4½ mm needles.

TENSION

On No. 4½mm needles, 19 sts and 25 rows to 10cm over stocking stitch.

ABBREVIATIONS

K knit; **P** purl; **sts** stitches; **tog** together; **inc** increase; **dec** decrease; **yfwd** yarn forward; **M1** make a stitch by picking up horizontal loop lying before next stitch and working into back of it; **patt** pattern; **rep** repeat; **alt** alternate; **cm** centimetres; **in** inches; **mm** millimetres.

BACK

With No. 3¼mm needles, cast on 86[92,96,102,106] sts and work in K1, P1 rib for 7cm.
Next row – Rib 4[7,4,7,9] sts, (M1, rib 7[7,8,8,8]) 11 times, M1, rib to end. *98[104,108,114,118] sts.*

Change to No. 4½mm needles and, starting with a K row, work in stocking stitch until Back measures 40cm, ending with a P row.
Next row – K3, P4, K to last 7 sts, P4, K3.
Next row – P. **
Rep last 2 rows until Back measures 66[67,68,69,70]cm, ending with a P row.

Shape shoulders by casting off 11[11,12,13,14] sts at beg of next 2 rows, then 11[12,12,13,13] sts at beg of following 4 rows.
Leave remaining 32[34,36,36,38] sts on a spare needle.

FRONT

Work as for Back to **.
Rep last 2 rows until Front measures 59[60,61,61,62]cm, ending with a P row.

Keeping border patt correct, **divide for neck** as follows:
Next row – Patt 38[40,41,44,45] sts, K2 tog, turn and leave remaining sts on a spare needle.
Continue on these 39[41,42,45,46] sts for first side and dec 1 st at neck edge on next 4 rows. Work 1 row. Now dec 1 st at neck edge on next and following alt row. *33[35,36,39,40] sts.*
Work straight until Front matches Back to shoulder, ending with a P row.

Shape shoulder by casting off 11[11,12,13,14] sts at beg of next row, then 11[12,12,13,13] sts at beg of following 2 rows.
With right side facing, leave centre 18[20,22,22,24] sts on a length of yarn, rejoin yarn to remaining sts, K2 tog, patt to end.
Finish to match first side, reversing shapings.

SLEEVES

With No. 3¼mm needles, cast on 42[44,44,46,48] sts and work in K1, P1 rib for 5cm.
Next row – Rib 3[4,4,5,6] sts, (M1, rib 4) 9 times, M1, rib to end. *52[54,54,56,58] sts.*

Change to No. 4½mm needles and, starting with a K row, work in stocking stitch, shaping sides by inc 1 st at each end of

next[5th,7th,7th,3rd] and every
following 7th[6th,5th,5th,5th] row
until there are 78[82,86,88,92] sts.
Work a few rows straight, if
required, until sleeve measures 40cm
down centre, ending with a P row.
Now inc 1 st at each end of next and
following 6 alt rows.
92[96,100,102,106] sts.

Next row – P.
Next row – Inc in first st,
K6[6,6,7,7] sts, P2, *K2, P2; rep
from * to last 7[7,7,8,8] sts,
K6[6,6,7,7] sts, inc in last st.
Next row – P8[8,8,9,9] sts, K2, *P2,
K2; rep from * to last 8[8,8,9,9] sts,
P to end.
Next row – Inc in first st,
K7[7,7,8,8] sts, P2, *K2, P2; rep
from * to last 8[8,8,9,9] sts,

K7[7,7,8,8], inc in last st.
Next row – P9[9,9,10,10] sts, K2,
*P2, K2; rep from * to last
9[9,9,10,10] sts, P to end.
Next row – Inc in first st,
K8[8,8,9,9], P2, *K2, P2; rep from *
to last 9[9,9,10,10] sts, K8[8,8,9,9],
inc in last st. Cast off.

TO MAKE UP

With wrong side of work facing,
block each piece by pinning out
round edges, and, omitting ribbing,
press parts lightly following
instructions on yarn labels.
Join right shoulder seam.

NECKBAND
With right side facing and No. 3¼

mm needles, knit up 18[18,18,20,20]
sts down left side of neck,
K18[20,22,22,24] sts from centre,
knit up 18[18,18,20,20] sts up right
side, K32[34,36,36,38] sts from back.
86[90,94,98,102] sts.
Work 11 rows in K1, P1 rib.
Next row – K1, *yfwd, K2 tog; rep
from * to last st, P1.
Work a further 11 rows K1, P1 rib.
Cast off loosely in rib.

Join neckband and left shoulder
seam.
Place centre of sleeve tops to
shoulder seams, then sew sleeve tops
to side edges of back and front.
Join side and sleeve seams.
Fold neckband in half at row of holes
to wrong side, and slip hem lightly
in position all round.

MATERIALS

Pair each Nos 3¼mm and 4½mm
needles.
Cable needle.
10 buttons.

TENSION

On No. 4½mm needles, 19 sts and
25 rows to 10cm over stocking stitch.

ABBREVIATIONS

K knit; **P** purl; **sts** stitches;
inc increase; **yfwd** yarn forward;
M1 make a stitch by picking up the
horizontal loop lying before the next
stitch and working into the back of
it; **tbl** through back of loops;
Cr2B slip next stitch on to cable
needle to back of work, K1 tbl, then
P stitch from cable needle; **Cr2F** slip
next stitch on cable needle to front of
work, P1, then K1 tbl, from cable
needle; **MB** make bobble – (K1,
yfwd, K1, yfwd, K1) all in next st,
K1 turn, P5 turn, K5 turn, P5, slip
2nd, 3rd, 4th, and 5th sts over first
st, turn, K bobble st tbl;
beg beginning; **patt** pattern;
rep repeat; **cm** centimetres;
in inches; **mm** millimetres.

BACK

With No. 3¼mm needles, cast on
96[106] sts, and work in K1, P1 rib
for 9cm.
Next row – Rib 3[8], (M1, rib 10) 9
times, M1, rib to end. *106[116] sts.*

Change to No. 4½mm needles.
Starting with a K row, work in
stocking stitch until Back measures
46cm, ending with a P row.

Shape armholes by casting off 4 sts
at beg of next 2 rows. *98[108] sts.*

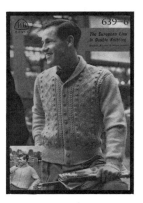

L E O

TRADITIONAL
MAN'S ARAN
JACKET WITH
ROLL COLLAR

*Warm, comfortable,
immensely stylish and
not too difficult to
knit. The classic
answer to every
sporting occasion.*

1 9 5 7

To fit chest		
cm	97–102	107–112
in	38–40	42–44

Garment measures		
cm	112	122
in	44	48

Length from top of shoulders		
cm	70	71
in	27½	28

Sleeve seam		
cm	49	49
in	19½	19½

Patons Diploma Aran

50g balls	17	18

Continue straight until Back
measures 70[71]cm, ending with a P
row.
Shape shoulders by casting off
32[36] sts at beg of next 2 rows. Cast
off remaining 34[36] sts.

PANEL PATT A (9 sts) FOR FRONT

1st row (right side) – slip next 3 sts
on cable needle to back of work, K1,
then K3 from cable needle, K1, slip
next st on cable needle to front of
work, K3, then K1 from cable needle.
2nd row – P.
3rd row – K.
4th row – P.
These 4 rows form panel patt A.

PANEL PATT B (33 sts) FOR FRONT

1st row (right side) – K6, P1, K4,
(K1 tbl, P1) 5 times, K1 tbl, K4, P1,
K6.
2nd row – P6, K1, P4, (P1 tbl, K1) 5
times, P1 tbl, P4, K1, P6.
3rd row – K6, P1, K3, Cr2B 3 times,
K1, Cr2F 3 times, K3, P1, K6.
4th row – P6, K1, P3, (P1 tbl, K1) 3
times, P1, K1, (P1 tbl, K1) twice, P1
tbl, P3, K1, P6.
5th row – K2, MB, K2, P1, K2,
Cr2B 3 times, K1, P1, K1, Cr2F 3
times, K2, P1, K2, MB, K2.
6th row – P6, K1, P2, (P1 tbl, K1) 3
times, (P1, K1) twice, (P1 tbl, K1)
twice, P1 tbl, P2, K1, P6.
7th row – K6, P1, K1, Cr2B 3 times,
(K1, P1) twice, K1, Cr2F 3 times, K1,
P1, K6.
8th row – P6, K1, P1, (P1 tbl, K1) 3
times, (P1, K1) 3 times, (P1 tbl, K1)
twice, P1 tbl, P1, K1, P6.
9th row – K6, P1, Cr2B 3 times,

(K1, P1) 3 times, K1, Cr2F 3 times, P1, K6.

10th row – P6, K1, (P1 tbl, K1) 3 times, (P1, K1) 4 times, (P1, tbl, K1) 3 times, P6.

11th row – K6, P1, slip next st on cable needle to front of work, K1, then K1 tbl, from cable needle, Cr2F twice, (P1, K1) 3 times, P1, Cr2B twice, slip next st on cable needle to back of work, K1 tbl, then K1 from cable needle, P1, K6.

12th row – P6, K1, P1, (P1 tbl, K1) 3 times, (P1, K1) 3 times, (P1 tbl, K1) twice, P1 tbl, P1, K1, P6.

13th row – K2, MB, K2, P1, K1, slip next st on cable needle to front of work, K1, then K1 tbl from cable needle, Cr2F twice, (P1, K1) twice, P1, Cr2B twice, slip next st on cable needle to back of work, K1 tbl, then K1 from cable needle, K1, P1, K2, MB, K2.

14th row – P6, K1, P2, (P1 tbl, K1) 3 times, (P1, K1) twice, (P1 tbl, K1) twice, P1 tbl, P2, K1, P6.

15th row – K6, P1, K2, slip next st on cable needle to front of work, K1, then K1 tbl from cable needle, Cr2F twice, P1, K1, P1, Cr2B twice, slip next st on cable needle to back of work, K1 tbl, then K1 from cable needle, K2, P1, K6.

16th row – P6, K1, P3, (P1 tbl, K1) 3 times, P1, K1, (P1 tbl, K1) twice, P1 tbl, P3, K1, P6.

17th row – K6, P1, K3, slip next st on cable needle to front of work, K1, then K1 tbl from cable needle, Cr2F twice, P1, Cr2B twice, slip next st on cable needle to back of work, K1 tbl, then K1 from cable needle, K3, P1, K6.

18th row – P6, K1, P4, (P1 tbl, K1) 5 times, P1 tbl, P4, K1, P6.

These 18 rows form panel patt B.

LEFT FRONT

With No. 3¼mm needles, cast on 48[52] sts and work in K1, P1 rib for 9cm.
Next row – Rib 4[5], (M1, rib 3) 13[14] times, M1, rib to end. *62[67] sts*.

Change to No. 4½mm needles and place patt as follows:
1st row (right side) – K4[9], P2, panel patt A 1st row, P2, panel patt B 1st row, P2, panel patt A 1st row, P1.
2nd row – K1, panel patt A 2nd row, K2, panel patt B 2nd row, K2, panel patt A 2nd row, K2, P4[9].
Continue thus until Front measures 46cm, ending with right side facing for next row.

Shape armhole by casting off 4 sts at beg of next row. *58[63] sts*.
Continue in patt until Front measures 53[54]cm, ending with right side facing for next row.

Keeping patt correct, **shape neck** by dec 1 st at end of next and every alt row until 38[42] sts remain.
Continue in patt until Front matches Back at shoulder, ending with *wrong* side facing for next row.
Next row – Patt 2, (work 2 tog, patt 4[5] 5 times, work 2 tog, patt to end. *32[36] sts*.
Cast off.

RIGHT FRONT

Work as for Left Front, reversing shapings and noting that patt will be placed as follows:
1st row (right side) – P1, panel patt A 1st row, P2, panel patt B 1st row, P2, panel patt A 1st row, P2, K4[9].
2nd row – P4[9], K2, panel patt A 2nd row, K2, panel patt B 2nd row, K2, panel patt A 2nd row, K1.

SLEEVES

With No. 3¼mm needles, cast on 44[48] sts and work in K1, P1 rib for 6cm.
Next row – Rib 4[6], (M1, rib 4) 9 times, M1, rib to end. *54[58] sts*.

Change to No. 4½mm needles; starting with a K row, work in stocking stitch, shaping sides by inc 1 st at each end of 5th and every following 6th row, until there are 88[92] sts.
Work straight until sleeve seam measures 51cm, ending with a P row.
Shape top by casting off 8[9] sts at beg of next 8 rows. Cast off remaining sts.

TO MAKE UP

With wrong side of work facing, block each piece by pinning out round edges and, omitting ribbing, press parts lightly following instructions on the yarn label, taking care not to spoil patt. Join shoulder seams. Sew cast off sleeve edges to armhole edges of back and fronts, then sew cast off armhole sts to top parts of sleeve side edges. Join side and sleeve seams.

RIGHT FRONT BORDER AND COLLAR

With No. 3¼mm needles cast on 9 sts and work as follows:
1st row (right side) – K2, (P1, K1) 3 times, K1.
2nd row – (K1, P1) 4 times, K1.
Rep last 2 rows until border, when slightly stretched, fits up right front edge to start of neck shaping, ending with a 2nd row.
Shape collar as follows:
1st row – K1, M1, (K1, P1) 3 times, K1, M1, K1.
2nd row – K2, (P1, K1) 3 times, P1, K2.
3rd row – *K1, P1; rep from * to last st, M1, K1.
4th row – K1, *P1, K1; rep from * to last st, K1.
5th row – *K1, P1; rep from * to last 2 sts, K1, M1, K1.
6th row – K1, *K1, P1; rep from * to last 2 sts, K2.
Rep 3rd to 6th rows until there are 31 sts, ending with 6th row.
Next 2 rows – In rib.
Next 2 rows – Rib to last 2 sts, turn and rib back.
Next 4 rows – In rib.
Rep last 6 rows until neck edge of collar reaches the centre back of neck. Cast off evenly in rib. Sew in position.

LEFT FRONT BORDER AND COLLAR

Work as for right front border, reversing collar shapings and with the addition of 10 buttonholes, the first to come 1cm above lower edge, the tenth 1cm below start of collar shaping and the remainder spaced evenly between.
First mark position of buttons on right border with pins to ensure even spacing, then work holes to correspond.

To make a buttonhole: 1st row (right side) – Rib 3, cast off next 2, rib to end; 2nd row – Rib, casting on 2 sts over those cast off.

Join collar edges at centre back neatly.
Sew on buttons. Press seams.

MATERIALS

Oddments of three contrasting yarns for embroidery.
Pair each No. 3³⁄₄mm and No. 4mm needles.
9 buttons.

TENSION

On No. 4mm needles, 22 sts and 30 rows to 10cm over reverse stocking stitch.

ABBREVIATIONS

K knit; **P** purl; **st** stitch; **tog** together; **inc** increase; **dec** decrease; **beg** beginning; **alt** alternate; **rep** repeat; **patt** pattern; **cm** centimetres; **in** inches; **mm** millimetres; **MB** make a bobble as follows – K1, P1, K1, P1, into next st, turn, P4 turn, K4 turn, P2 tog twice, turn, K2 tog.

BOBBLE PATT

(worked over 12 sts)
1st row (right side) – MB, P10, MB.
2nd and every alt row – K.
3rd row – P.
5th row – P1, MB, P8, MB, P1.
7th row – P.
9th row – P2, MB, P6, MB, P2.
11th row – P.
13th row – P3, MB, P4, MB, P3.
14th row – K.
These 14 rows form bobble patt.

BACK

With No. 3³⁄₄mm needles, cast on 98[108] sts and work in rib as follows:
1st row (right side) – K3, *P2, K3; rep from * to end.
2nd row – P3, *K2, P3; rep from * to end.

HEIDI

WOMAN'S
TYROLEAN
EMBROIDERED
CARDIGAN

Pine forests, and thoughts of hot chocolate, as you drift off the slopes – into something infinitely more feminine.

---

1 9 4 9

To fit bust		
cm	81–86	91–97
in	32–34	36–38
Garment measures		
cm	89	100
in	35	39½
Length from shoulders		
cm	57	58
in	22½	23
Sleeve length		
cm	43	44
in	17	17½
Patons Diploma DK		
50g balls	11	12

Rep these 2 rows for 9cm, ending with a 2nd row.

Change to No. 4mm needles and work in rib and patt as follows:
1st row (right side) – P5[10], rib 88, P5[10].
2nd row – K5[10], rib 88, K5[10].
3rd row – P10[15], rib 78, P10[15].
4th row – K10[15], rib 78, K10[15].
5th row – P15[20], rib 68, P15[20].
6th row – K15[20], rib 68, K15[20].
7th row – P4[9], bobble patt 12 sts as 1st row of bobble instructions, P4, rib 58, P4, bobble patt 12 sts as 1st row, P4[9].
8th row – K20[25], rib 58, K20[25].
9th row – P25[30], rib 48, P25[30].
10th row – K25[30], rib 48, K25[30].
11th row – P4[9], bobble patt 12 as 5th row, P14, rib 38, P14, bobble patt 12 as 5th row, P4[9].
12th row – K30[35], rib 38, K30[35].
13th row – P35[40], rib 28, P35[40].
14th row – K35[40], rib 28, K35[40].
15th row – P4[9], bobble patt 12 as 9th row, P24, rib 18, P24, bobble patt 12 as 9th row, P4[9].
16th row – K40[45], rib 19, K40[45].
17th row – P45[50], K3, P2, K3, P45[50].
18th row – K45[50], P3, K2, P3, K45[50].
19th row – P4[9], bobble patt 12 as 13th row, P66, bobble patt 12 as 13th row, P4[9].
20th row – K to end.
Continue in *reverse* stocking stitch, placing bobble patt as follows:
Starting with a P row, work 6 rows.
Next row – P17[22], (bobble patt 12 as 1st row, P14) 3 times, P to end.
Next row – K to end.
Continue working appropriate rows of bobble patt until the 14th row has been worked.
Work 6 rows.

Next row – P4[9], (bobble patt 12 as 1st row, P14) 3 times, bobble patt 12 as 1st row, P to end.
Next row – K to end.
Continue working appropriate rows of bobble patt until the 14th row has been worked.
Work 6 rows.
Next row – P17[22], (bobble patt 12 as 1st row, P14) 3 times, P to end.
Next row – K to end.
Continue working bobble patt until the 12th row of bobble patt has been worked.

Shape armholes:
Next row – Cast off 4[6] sts, patt to end.
Next row – Cast off 4[6] sts, K to end.
Work 6 rows dec 1 st at each end of next and following 2 alt rows.
Next row – P2 tog, P21[24], (bobble patt 12 as 1st row, P14) twice, P to last 2 sts, P2 tog.
Next row – K to end.
Continue working bobble patt, *at the same time* dec 1 st at each end of next and following 3 alt rows. *74[80] sts.*
Work 5 more rows to complete bobble patt.
Work 6 rows.
Next row – P5[8], (bobble patt 12 as 1st row, P14) twice, bobble patt 12 as 1st row, P to end.
Next row – K to end.
Continue working bobble patt until the 14th row has been worked.
Work 6 rows.

Next row – P18[21], (bobble patt 12 as 1st row, P14) twice, P to end.
Next row – K to end.
Continue working bobble patt until the 14th row has been worked.
Work 4[8] rows.

Shape shoulders by casting off 7 sts at beg of next 4 rows, then 7[8] sts at beg of following 2 rows.
Cast off remaining 32[36] sts.

LEFT FRONT

With No. 3¾/4mm needles, cast on 50[55] sts and work in rib as follows:
1st row (right side) – *K3, P2; rep from * to end.

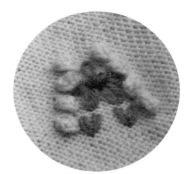

2nd row – *K2, P3; rep from * to end.
Rep these 2 rows for 9cm, ending with a 2nd row.

Change to No. 4mm needles and work in patt as follows:

1st row (right side) – P5[10], rib 45.
2nd row – Rib 45, K5[10].
3rd row – P10[15], rib 40.
4th row – Rib 40, K10[15].
5th row – P15[20], rib 35.
6th row – Rib 35, K15[20].
7th row – P4[9], bobble patt 12 as 1st row, P4, rib 30.
8th row – Rib 30, K20[25].

9th row – P25[30], rib 25.
10th row – Rib 25, K25[30].
11th row – P4[9], bobble patt 12 as 5th row, P14, rib 20.
12th row – Rib 20, K30[35].
13th row – P35[40], rib 15.
14th row – Rib 15, K35[40].
15th row – P4[9], bobble patt 12 as 9th row, P24, rib 10.

16th row – Rib 10, K40[45].
17th row – P45[50], K3, P2.
18th row – K2, P3, K45[50].
19th row – P4[9], bobble patt 12 as 13th row, P34.
20th row – K to end.
Work 6 rows.
Next row – P17[22], bobble patt 12 as 1st row, P to end.
Next row – K to end.
Continue working bobble patt until the 14th row has been worked.
Work 6 rows.

Next row – P4[9], bobble patt 12 as 1st row, P14, bobble patt 12 as 1st row, P to end.
Next row – K to end.
Continue working bobble patt until the 14th row has been worked.
Work 6 rows.
Next row – P17[22], bobble patt 12 as 1st row, P to end.
Next row – K to end.
Continue working bobble patt until the 12th row of bobble patt has been worked.

Shape armhole:
Next row – Cast off 4[6] sts, patt to end.
Next row – K to end.
Work 6 rows dec 1 st at *beginning* of next and following 2 alt rows.
Next row – P2 tog, P21[24], bobble patt 12 as 1st row, P to end.

Next row – K to end.
Continue working bobble patt, *at the same time* dec 1 st at beg of next and following 3 alt rows at armhole edge. *38[41] sts.*
Work 5 more rows to complete bobble patt.
Work 6 rows.
Next row – P5[8], bobble patt 12 as 1st row, P to end.
Next row – K to end.

Continue working bobble patt until the 14th row has been worked.
Work 6 rows.
Next row – P18[21], bobble patt 12 as 1st row, P to end.
Next row – K to end.
Keeping continuity of bobble patt, work 1[3] rows ending with *wrong* side facing for next row.

Shape neck by casting off 4 sts at beg of next row.

Dec 1 st at neck edge on every row until 21[22] sts remain.
Work 1 row, ending with right side facing for next row.

Shape shoulder by casting off 7 sts at beg of next and following alt row. Work 1 row. Cast off remaining 7[8] sts.

RIGHT FRONT

With No. 3¾mm needles, cast on 50[55] sts and work in rib as follows:
1st row (right side) – *P2, K3; rep from * to end.
2nd row – *P3, K2; rep from * to end.
Rep these 2 rows for 9cm, ending with a 2nd row.

Change to No. 4mm needles and work in patt as follows:
1st row – Rib 45, P5[10].

2nd row – K5[10], rib 45.
3rd row – Rib 40, P10[15].
4th row – K10[15], rib 40.
5th row – Rib 35, P15[20].

6th row – K15[20], rib 35.
7th row – Rib 30, P4, bobble patt 12 as 1st row, P4[9].
8th row – K20[25], rib 30.
9th row – Rib 25, P25[30].
10th row – K25[30], rib 25.

11th row – Rib 20, P14, bobble patt 12 as 5th row, P4[9].
12th row – K30[35], rib 20.
13th row – Rib 15, P35[40].
14th row – K35[40], rib 15.
15th row – Rib 10, P24, bobble patt 12 as 9th row, P4[9].

16th row – K40[45], rib 10.
17th row – P2, K3, P45[50].
18th row – K45[50], P3, K2.
19th row – P34, bobble patt 12 as

13th row, P4[9].
20th row – K to end.
Work 6 rows.

Next row – P21, bobble patt 12 as
1st row, P to end.
Next row – K to end.
Continue working bobble patt until
the 14th row has been worked.
Work 6 rows.
Next row – P8, bobble patt 12 as 1st
row, P14, bobble patt 12 as 1st row,
P to end.
Next row – K to end.

Continue working bobble patt until
the 14th row has been worked.
Work 6 rows.
The last 40 rows set the position of
bobble patt.

Keeping continuity of patt, complete
to match Left Front, reversing
shapings.

SLEEVES

With No. 3¾mm needles, cast on
42[48] sts and work 7[11] rows in
garter stitch (every row K).

Change to No. 4mm needles and,
starting with a P row, work 8 rows
in reverse stocking stitch.
Inc 1 st at each end of next row.
Work 3 rows.
Next row – P3[6], bobble patt 12 as
1st row, P14, bobble patt 12 as 1st
row, P to end.

Next row – K to end.
Work 12 more rows of bobble patt,
at the same time inc 1 st at each end
of the next and every following 6th
row.
Inc 1 st at each end of next row.
Work 5 rows.
Next row – Inc in first st, P18[21],
bobble patt 12 as 1st row, P18[21],
inc in last st.

Next row – K to end.
Work 12 more rows of bobble patt,
inc 1 st at each end of every 6th row
from previous inc. *56[62] sts.*
Continue in patt as set, working 6
rows between each bobble patt and
inc 1 st at each end of every 6th row
as before until there are 76[82] sts,
taking inc sts into bobble patt.
Work a further 21 rows, ending with
a 14th row of patt.

Keeping continuity of patt, **shape
top** by casting off 4[6] sts at beg of
next 2 rows.
Dec 1 st at each end of next and
every following 4th row until 62[64]
sts remain.
Work 1 row.
Dec 1 st at each end of next and
every alt row until 22 sts remain.
Cast off.

TO MAKE UP – FRONT BORDERS AND NECK TRIM

Do not press.
Join shoulder and side seams.

BUTTON BORDER

With No. 3¾mm needles, cast on 7
sts and work in garter stitch (every
row K) until border when slightly
stretched fits up left front to neck
edge. Sew in position as you go
along. Cast off.

BUTTONHOLE BORDER

Work as for button border with the
addition of 9 buttonholes, the first to
come 1cm up from lower edge, the
last 1cm from neck edge and the
remainder spaced evenly between.
First mark position of buttons on
button border with pins to ensure
even spacing, then work buttonholes
to correspond.

To make a buttonhole: 1st row
(right side) – K3, cast off 2, K to
end; 2nd row – K, casting on 2 over
those cast off.

NECK BORDER

With No. 3¾mm needles, cast on 7
sts and work in garter stitch until
strip measures sufficient to fit round
neck edge, sew in position as you go
along around neck. Cast off.

NECK TRIM

With No. 3¾mm needles, cast on 5
sts and work 78cm in stocking stitch.
Cast off.
Gather strip by running a thread
through centre, draw up evenly to
form a ruching and sew round neck
border.

Join sleeve seams and insert sleeves.
Embroider daisies and leaves in
centre of bobble patts, 4 on each
front, 3 at top of each sleeve and 4
across top of back. See photograph.
Sew on buttons.

MATERIALS
Pair each No. 3¼mm and No. 4mm needles.
15 buttons.

TENSION
On No. 4mm needles, 22 sts and 30 rows to 10cm over stocking stitch.

ABBREVIATIONS
K knit; **P** purl; **sts** stitches; **tog** together; **inc** increase; **dec** decrease; **M1** make a stitch by picking up horizontal loop lying before next stitch and working into back of it; **rep** repeat; **beg** beginning; **alt** alternate; **cm** centimetres; **in** inches; **mm** millimetres; **MS** main shade; **B** 1st contrast; **C** 2nd contrast.

BACK

With No. 3¼mm needles and MS, cast on 88[92,98,104,110] sts and work in K1, P1 rib and stripes of 2 rows MS, 2 rows B, 2 rows MS, 2 rows C, until 18 rows have been worked, ending with 2 rows in MS. Break off B and C.
Continue in MS as follows:
Next row – Rib 5[7,3,6,9] sts (M1, rib 7[6,7,7,7]) 11[13,13,13,13] times, M1, rib to end. *100[106,112,118,124] sts.*

Change to No. 4mm needles and, starting with a K row, work in stocking stitch until Back measures 42cm, ending with a P row.

Shape armholes by casting off 5 sts at beg of next 2 rows. *90[96,102,108,114] sts.*
Work straight until Back measures 62[63,64,65,65]cm, ending with a P row.

Shape shoulders by casting off

ETHEL

WOMAN'S LUMBER-JACKET WITH STRIPED COLLAR, CUFFS AND WELT

Elegant, easy to wear, great style!

1 9 2 4

To fit bust					
cm	81	86	91	97	102
in	32	34	36	38	40

Garment measures					
cm	92	98	103	109	114
in	36	38½	40½	43	45

Length from top of shoulders					
cm	62	63	64	65	65
in	24½	25	25	25½	25½

Sleeve seam					
cm	46	46	47	47	47
in	18	18	18½	18½	18½

Patons Beehive DK

Main shade (MS)					
50g balls	7	7	8	8	9
1st contrast (B)					
50g balls	1	1	1	1	1
2nd contrast (C)					
50g balls	1	1	1	1	1

29[31,34,36,38] sts at beg of next 2 rows.
Leave remaining 32[34,34,36,38] sts on a spare needle.

LEFT FRONT

With No. 3¼mm needles and MS, cast on 44[46,48,52,54] sts and work 18 rows in rib as for Back.
Continue in MS as follows:
Next row – Rib 4[5,3,5,6] sts, (M1, rib 7[6,6,7,6]) 5[6,7,6,7] times, M1, rib to end. *50[53,56,59,62] sts.*

Change to No. 4mm needles and, starting with a K row, work in stocking stitch until Front measures 42cm, ending with a P row.

Shape armhole by casting off 5 sts at beg of next row. *45[48,51,54,57] sts.*
Continue straight until Front measures 56[57,58,59,59]cm, ending with a P row.

Shape neck as follows:
Next row – K to last 10[11,11,12,13] sts, K2 tog, turn and leave remaining sts on a safety-pin.
Dec 1 st at neck edge on next 4 rows.
Work 1 row.
Now dec 1 st at neck edge on next and following 2 alt rows. *29[31,34,36,38] sts.*
Work a few rows straight until Front matches Back to shoulder. Cast off.

RIGHT FRONT

Work as for Left Front, reversing shapings.

SLEEVES

With No. 3¼mm needles and MS, cast on 42[44,44,46,46] sts and work

18 rows in rib as for Back.
Continue in MS as follows:
Next row – Rib 2[3,3,4,4] sts, (M1, rib 2) 19 times, M1, rib to end. *62[64,64,66,66] sts.*

Change to No. 4mm needles and, starting with a K row, work in stocking stitch, shaping sides by inc 1 st at each end of 5th[9th,9th,3rd,3rd] and every following 8th[7th,6th,6th,6th] row until there are 88[92,96,102,102] sts.
Work straight until sleeve seam measures 48[48,49,49,49]cm, ending with a P row.

Shape top by casting off 8 sts at beg of next 10 rows.
Cast off remaining 8[12,16,22,22] sts.

TO MAKE UP

Do not press.
Join shoulder seams. Place centre of sleeve tops to shoulder seams, then sew sleeve tops to armhole edges of Back and Fronts. Sew cast-off armhole sts to sleeve sides. Join side and sleeve seams.

NECKBAND

With right side facing, No. 3¼mm needles and MS, K8[9,9,10,11] sts from Right Front, knit up 16 sts up right side of neck, K32[34,34,36,38] sts from Back, dec 1 st at centre, knit up 16 sts down left side, then

K8[9,9,10,11] sts from Left Front. *79[83,83,87,91] sts.*
Now work in K1, P1 rib (rows on *wrong* side having a K1 at each end), and working in stripes of 1 row MS, 2 rows C, 2 rows MS, 2 rows B, 1 row MS.
Rep last 8 rows once more.
Cast off evenly in rib and MS.

LEFT FRONT BORDER

With No. 3¼mm needles and MS, cast on 9 sts and work as follows:
1st row (right side) – K2, (P1, K1) 3 times, K1.
2nd row – K1, (P1, K1) 4 times.
Rep last 2 rows until border, when slightly stretched, fits up left front to top of neckband, sewing in position as you go along.

RIGHT FRONT BORDER

Work as for left border, with the addition of 15 buttonholes, the first to come 1cm above lower edge, the fifteenth 1cm below top of neckband, and the remainder spaced evenly between.
First mark position of buttons on left front with pins to ensure even spacing, then work holes to correspond.

To make a buttonhole: 1st row (right side) – Rib 4, cast off next 2, rib to end. 2nd row – Rib, casting on 2 sts over those cast off.

Sew on buttons.

LEGWARMERS

MATERIALS

8 50g balls of **Patons Beehive Chunky**.
Pair of No. 6½mm needles.

MEASUREMENTS

Length with cuffs turned over, 69cm (27in); width at top of leg when slightly stretched, 49cm (19½in).

TENSION

On No. 6½mm needles, 21 sts and 28 rows to 15cm over stocking stitch.

ABBREVIATIONS

K knit; **P** purl; **st** stitch; **inc** increase; **rep** repeat; **cm** centimetres; **in** inches; **mm** millimetres.

With No. 6½mm needles, cast on 39 sts and work in rib as follows:
1st row (right side) – K1, *P1, K1; rep from * to end.
2nd row – P1, *K1, P1; rep from * to end.
Rep these 2 rows until work measures 13cm, ending with a 2nd row.
Continue in rib and shape by inc 1 st at each end of next and every following 4th row until there are 59 sts, taking inc sts into rib.
Continue straight in rib until work measures 42cm, ending with right side facing for next row.
Now inc 1 st at each end of next and every 4th row until there are 87 sts.
Continue straight until work measures 81cm.

JOANNA

LEGWARMERS AND HAT

For blackberrying, blueberrying, picking holly . . .

1 9 7 0

Cast off loosely in rib. Make another in the same way.

TO MAKE UP

Join back seam, reversing seam at top and lower edge for 6cm for turn-backs.
Fold cuffs to right side.

HAT

MATERIALS

2 50g balls **Patons Beehive Chunky**.
Pair No. 6½mm needles.

MEASUREMENTS

Average head size.

TENSION

On No. 6½mm needles, 21 sts and 28 rows to 15cm over stocking stitch.

ABBREVIATIONS

K knit; **P** purl; **st** stitch; **sl** slip; **tog** together; **psso** pass slipped stitch over; **rep** repeat; **cm** centimetres; **mm** millimetres.

With No. 6½mm needles, cast on 78 sts and work in rib as follows:
Next row (right side) – *P1, K1; rep from * to end.
Rep this row until work measures 32cm, ending with right side facing for next row.

Shape crown as follows:
Next row – *P1, K1, P1, sl 1, K2 tog, psso; rep from * to end. *52 sts.*
Work 3 rows in P1, K1 rib.
Next row – sl 1, K1, psso, *P1, sl 1, K2 tog, psso; rep from * to last 2 sts, sl 1, K1, psso. *26 sts.*
Work 3 rows in K1, P1 rib.
Next row – *sl 1, K1, psso; rep from * to end. *13 sts.*
Break off yarn, thread through remaining sts, draw up tightly and fasten off securely.

TO MAKE UP

Join back seam, reversing seam at lower edge for turn-back.
Fold back brim to right side, then fold back again as required to form a double brim.

P E R C Y

MAN'S LONG-SLEEVED PULLOVER

A unique sweater from the twenties. It takes easily to a variety of colour combinations. Definitely not for beginners.

1 9 2 2

To fit chest				
cm	97	102	107	112
in	38	40	42	44

Length from top of shoulders				
cm	65	67	68	68
in	25½	26½	27	27

Sleeve length, with cuff turned back				
cm	46	47	47	48
in	18	18½	18½	19

Patons Clansman DK

Shade A	50g balls	8	8	9	9
Shade B	50g balls	7	7	8	8

MATERIALS

Pair each No. 3¼mm and No. 4mm needles.

TENSION

On No. 4mm needles, 26 sts and 26 rows to 10cm over patt.

ABBREVIATIONS

K knit; **P** purl; **st** stitch; **tog** together; **inc** increase; **dec** decrease; **beg** beginning; **alt** alternate; **rep** repeat; **patt** pattern; **cm** centimetres; **in** inches; **mm** millimetres; **M1** make a stitch by picking up horizontal loop lying before next stitch and working into back of it; **A** main shade; **B** contrast shade.

NOTE

When working in patt from chart, strand yarn not in use loosely across wrong side of work over not more than 3 sts at a time to keep fabric elastic.
Read odd rows K from right to left and even rows P from left to right.

BACK

** With No. 3¼mm needles and A, cast on 111[117,123,129] sts and work in rib as follows:
1st row (right side) – K1, *P1, K1; rep from * to end.
2nd row – P1, *K1, P1; rep from * to end.
Rep these 2 rows twice more, then 1st row again.
Next row – Rib 6[9,12,2], *M1, rib 4[4,4,5]; rep from * to last 5[8,11,2] sts, M1, rib to end. *137[143,149,155] sts.*

Change to No. 4mm needles, join in B and work in patt from chart (see p. 127), repeating the 34 patt sts 4 times across, working the first 0[3,6,9] sts and last 1[4,7,10] sts on K rows, and first 1[4,7,10] sts and last 0[3,6,9] sts in P rows as indicated.
Rep the 42 rows of patt until Back measures 41cm, ending with a P row.

Keeping continuity of patt, **shape armholes** by casting off 6 sts at beg of next 2 rows.
Dec 1 st at each end of next 3 rows, then every alt row until 105[109,113,117] sts remain.
Work straight until Back measures 65[67,68,68]cm, ending with a P row.

Shape shoulders by casting off 10[10,10,11] sts at beg of next 4 rows, then 9[10,11,10] sts at beg of following 2 rows.
Cast off remaining 47[49,51,53] sts.

POCKET LININGS

(work 2)
With No. 4mm needles and A, cast on 27 sts and, starting and ending with a K row, work 10cm in stocking stitch.
Next row – P4 (M1, P4) 4 times, M1, P3. *32 sts.*
Leave these sts on a spare needle.

FRONT

Work as for Back from ** until Front measures 13cm, ending with a P row.

Place pocket linings as follows:
Next row – Patt 10[10,12,12], *slip next 32 sts on to a length of yarn and in place of these sts patt across 32 sts of Pocket Lining*, patt

53[59,61,67], rep from * to *, patt
10[10,12,12].
Continue in patt until Front matches
Back to start of armhole shaping,
ending with a P row.

**Shape armhole and divide for
neck** as follows:
Next row – Cast off 6 sts, patt
51[54,57,60] (including st on needle
after cast off), turn, and leave
remaining sts on a spare needle.
Work in patt on these sts for first
side.
Work 1 row.
Dec 1 st at armhole edge of next 2
rows.
Dec 1 st at armhole edge of next and
following 7[8,9,10] alt rows. Work
5[5,5,3] rows.
Now dec 1 st at neck edge on next
and every following 3rd row until
29[30,31,32] sts remain.
Work a few rows straight until Front
matches Back to start of shoulder
shaping, ending with a P row.

Shape shoulder by casting off
10[10,10,11] sts at beg of next and
following alt row.
Work 1 row. Cast off remaining
9[10,11,10] sts.

With right side facing slip centre 23
sts on to a spare needle, rejoin yarn
to remaining sts, patt to end.
Complete to match first side,
reversing shapings.

SLEEVES

With No. 3¼mm needles and A,
cast on 51[51,53,55] sts and work
10cm in rib as for Back, ending with
a 1st row.
Next row – Rib 4[4,3,4], *M1, rib 2,
M1, rib 3; rep from * to last 2[2,0,1]
sts, rib to end. *69[69,73,75] sts.*

Change to No. 4mm needles. Join
B and work in patt from chart,
repeating the 34 patt sts twice,
working first 0[0,2,3] sts and last
1[1,3,4] sts on K rows, and first
1[1,3,4] sts and last 0[0,2,3] sts on P
rows as indicated, *at the same time*
shaping sides by inc 1 st at each end
of 5th and every following
6th[6th,5th,5th] row until there are
99[103,107,111] sts, taking inc sts
into patt.

Work straight until edge measures
51[52,52,53]cm, ending with a P
row.

Keeping continuity of patt, **shape
top** by casting off 6 sts, at beg of
next 2 rows.
Dec 1 st at each end of next and
every alt row until 53 sts remain.
Work 1 row.
Dec 1 st at each end of every row
until 27 sts remain.
Cast off.

TO MAKE UP –
POCKET TOPS AND
NECK BORDER

Press, following the instructions
given on the yarn bands.

POCKET TOPS

With right side facing, No. 3¼mm
needles and A, K across 32 sts of
Pockets, inc 1 st at centre.
1st row (wrong side) – P1, *K1, P1;
rep from * to end.
2nd row – K1, *P1, K1; rep from *
to end.

Rep these 2 rows twice more, then
1st row again. Cast off evenly in rib.
Join pocket tops neatly to right side
and pocket linings lightly to wrong
side.

Join shoulder seams.

NECK BORDER

With right side facing, No. 3¼mm
needles and A, K across 23 sts from
front neck.
Work 10 rows in rib as for pocket
tops until ribbing fits up to start of
neck shaping, and ending with *wrong*
side facing for next row.

Next row – Rib 11, cast off 1 st, rib
to end.
Next row – (K1, P1) 5 times, K1,
turn, leave remaining 11 sts on a
safety-pin.

Continue in rib on these 11 sts until
work is long enough to fit up side of
neck and round to centre back, sew
in position as you go along.
Cast off in rib.

With right side facing, rejoin yarn to
remaining 11 sts and complete to
match first side.
Join cast off sts at back neck.
Join side and sleeve seams. Insert
sleeves. Fold cuffs in half to right
side.
Press seams.

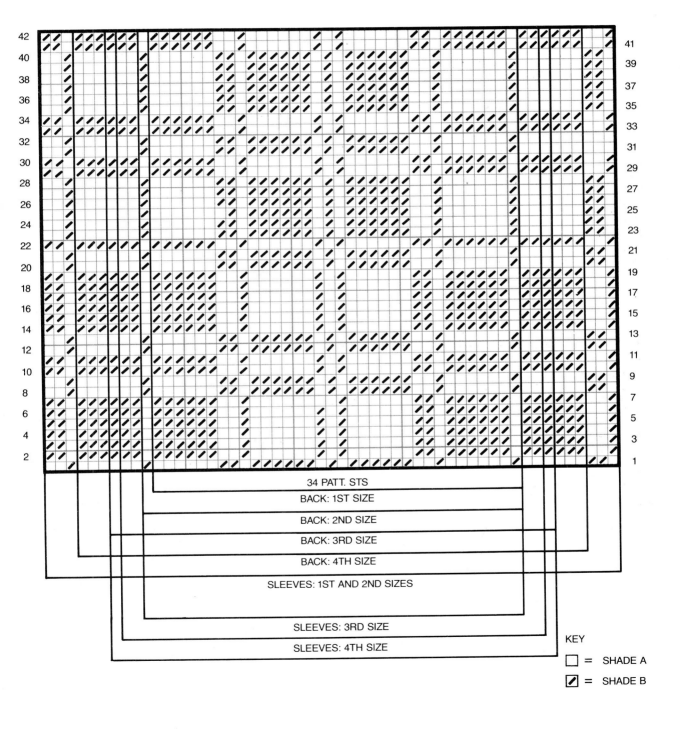

34 PATT. STS

BACK: 1ST SIZE

BACK: 2ND SIZE

BACK: 3RD SIZE

BACK: 4TH SIZE

SLEEVES: 1ST AND 2ND SIZES

SLEEVES: 3RD SIZE

SLEEVES: 4TH SIZE

KEY

☐ = SHADE A

▨ = SHADE B

ACKNOWLEDGEMENTS

Photographs: Jill Furmanovsky Associates; *Styling*: Erica Moore; *Make-up*: by Valerie MacDonald using Les Pastel range of cosmetics by Bourjois, Paris, London; *Hair*: by John Sparrowhawk at Sub, Monmouth St, London wc2.

THANKS TO everyone who gave or lent their time, energy, belongings and support.

Special thanks to: Sally Gaminara at Penguin Books for having enough faith to take on a second book.

THE TEAM: Jill Furmanovsky, Erica Moore, John Sparrowhawk, Valerie McDonald, Mike Prentice of Locations Unlimited, our Location Manager.

EVERYONE AT PATONS in Alloa, Darlington and London: especially Nan Govan in Alloa; John Morgans in Darlington; Sandra Cook and Joan Proudfoot, who transcribed the patterns; Rose Munir in London.

Ewart Sturrock, Sterts Arts Centre, Upton Cross, Liskeard, Cornwall; The National Trust for Cornwall; The National Maritime Trust; Roger Swingler and Bryan Preston, Photography Department, Plymouth College of Art Design, and students Katie Champion, Vicky Morrison and Jennie Morris who modelled for us; Virginia Bolton, photography assistant; our other models, Roger and Sam Jago, Ron Berglas, Tristan Sturrock, John Sparrowhawk, Laura Marshall and Emma Seal; George Carney of the Ford Motor Company for lending the wonderfully economical and elastic Sierra 2.0 GL Estate; Frances Hinchcliffe at the Textile Department, Victoria and Albert Museum, London; and a very special thank you to all our excellent knitters.

Men's hats, women's shorts and other accessories kindly loaned by Selfridges, London; women's hats kindly loaned by The Hat Shop, Neal Street, Covent Garden, London wc2; culottes by Sheridan Barnet; other garments kindly loaned from Patons Baldwins wardrobe; golfing accessories kindly loaned by The Shop, St Mellion Golf Club, Callington, Cornwall; shooting accessories kindly loaned by The Shop, Lower Lake Shooting Ground, Rilla Mill, Liskeard, Cornwall.

NEEDLE EQUIVALENTS

UK Metric	Former UK/Canadian	American	European Metric
$1\frac{3}{4}$ mm	15	–	–
2 mm	14	0	2
$2\frac{1}{4}$ mm	13	1	
$2\frac{3}{4}$ mm	12	2	$2\frac{1}{2}$
3 mm	11	–	3
$3\frac{1}{4}$ mm	10	3	
$3\frac{3}{4}$ mm	9	5	$3\frac{1}{2}$
4 mm	8	6	4
$4\frac{1}{2}$ mm	7	7	$4\frac{1}{2}$
5 mm	6	8	5
$5\frac{1}{2}$ mm	5	9	$5\frac{1}{2}$
6 mm	4	10	6
$6\frac{1}{2}$ mm	3	$10\frac{1}{2}$	$6\frac{1}{2}$
7 mm	2	–	7
$7\frac{1}{2}$ mm	1	–	$7\frac{1}{2}$
8 mm	0	11	8
9 mm	00	13	9
10 mm	000	15	10